Plato's Phaedo

PLATO'S
PHAEDO

With Translation,
Introduction and
Glossary

Eva Brann
Peter Kalkavage
Eric Salem

Focus Classical Library
Focus Publishing/R Pullins Company
Newburyport MA 01950

The Focus Philosophical Library

ISBN 10: 0-941051-69-2
ISBN 13: 978-0-941051-69-9

This book is published by Focus Publishing/R Pullins Company, PO Box 369, Newburyport MA 01950 All rights are reserved. No part of this publication may be produced, stored in a retrieval system, produced on stage or otherwise performed, transmitted by any means, electronic, mechanical, by photocopying, recording, or by any other media or means without the prior written permission of the publisher.

Cover Design: Catherine Dripps

Printed in the United States of America

10 9 8 7 6 5

1107TS

To Jacob Klein
1899-1978
Teacher at St. John's College, Annapolis
1938-1978

CONTENTS

PHAEDO

Introduction

In the first book of his *Inquiries*, Herodotus tells the story of Solon and Croesus. The Athenian wise man gives the Lydian tyrant a piece of advice. "Look to the end," he says, if you want to know whether a human life has really been blessed or happy. As he makes abundantly clear to Croesus, Solon means by end no more and no less than how a man has died.

If there is any truth to Solon's words, we would do well to pay close attention to the *Phaedo* in our pursuit of the question, "Who is Socrates, and was he blessed or happy?" In the *Phaedo* the philosopher Socrates "meets his end." He does so in the double sense of the phrase: He reaches the termination of his deathbound life, and he reflects, in the company of his friends, on the deathless intellectual vision to which his life had been devoted. To pay serious attention to the *Phaedo*, then, is to do more than investigate what Socrates talked about and did on the day he died. It is to pursue the question that underlies and pervades all the dialogues of Plato: Who is the true philosopher, and is he really the most blessed and happiest of men?

Like all the other Platonic dialogues, the *Phaedo* has its own setting, circumstances and limits. Socrates is a perpetual mystery, the perennial questionable questioner, and Plato is careful to present him, never "as such" or "in himself," but always in a continually shifting, and therefore life-like, context with an ever-varying set of interlocutors. The *Phaedo*, though revelatory as befits the story of an end, speaks from its own perspective and within its own confines. Like all the other dialogues, it has its share of concealment, unresolved perplexity, omissions, exaggerations and deliberately contrived "bad arguments" — all meant to make us think in ways we are left to discover for ourselves. The reader must steel himself to the fact that the story of Socrates' end will not easily or unproblematically open itself up to his gaze.

The *Phaedo* is the most poignant and personal of all the dialogues. The conversation is literally a matter of life and death as the soon-to-die Socrates, in the company of adoring and anxious friends, takes up the question of what happens to us at the moment of our death. But there is another poignancy to the *Phaedo:* Socrates here attempts to transform our worry about death into a reflection on what it means to be fully and truly *alive*, into a discursive hymn in praise of the philosophic life. This hymn is deeply perplexing. On the one hand, Socrates encourages both himself and his friends with the hope for a more-than-mortal life after the soul leaves the body. On the other hand, the means to this encouragement consist in giving arguments that are full of patent logical flaws. As noted above, we find such deliberate illogic in all the dialogues. But here the illogic has an especially perplexing and troubling character since what is at issue is nothing less than our individual selves. How are we to reconcile the strength of Socrates' encouragement with the weakness of the actual arguments? Granting that the *Phaedo* is most centrally about the praise of philosophy in its care for deathless being, what does Socrates actually think about the fate of the individual soul, *his soul*, at the moment of death? Where does the last conversation of Socrates leave us at the end?

The dialogue's opening word, "self" (*autos*), brings us to the very core of the mystery before us. Echecrates asks whether Phaedo *himself* was present at Socrates' death. The intensive pronoun is an excellent example of how the deepest philosophical problems for Plato tend to lie right at the surface of ordinary language. Echecrates' question makes us wonder what words like "himself" and "itself" ultimately mean, wonder what it means to *intensify identity*. Now here in the *Phaedo* and in other dialogues, those ultimate thinkables — the forms — are often referred to as "the things themselves all by themselves." Echecrates' opening question thus calls to mind not only the human self, of which "Phaedo himself" is an example, but also the forms. The *Phaedo*'s opening word "self" leads us directly to questions that are at the very heart of the dialogue: What is the soul? What is the relation between soul and form? And does our selfhood, our identity, make any sense without the body to which our soul is mysteriously attached?

The *Phaedo* belongs to the class of narrated or, to use Socrates' word, recollected Platonic dialogues. To the class of non-narrated or directly presented conversations belong dialogues like the *Meno* and *Gorgias*. Of the narrated sort, some are virtual soliloquies with an unidentified listener, like the *Republic* and *Parmenides*. Others are narrations embedded within a directly presented conversation. Dialogues that belong to this class include the postmortem recollections of Socrates: the *Symposium*, *Theaetetus* and *Phaedo*. Their very form compels us to ask: Why is it important to keep the memory of Socrates alive?

The *Phaedo*'s recollection of Socrates is a perplexing blend of *logos* and *mythos*, argument and story. As we hear early on, Socrates' death had been delayed — by "a bit of chance," as Phaedo says. Every year, the Athenians, in accordance with their vow to Apollo, send an embassy to Delos. Before this embassy returns to Athens, the city must keep itself pure and not put anyone to death. The embassy commemorates Theseus' rescue of the fourteen young Athenians (the Twice Seven, as Phaedo calls them, in keeping with the fact that the group was composed of both youths and maidens) from the Minotaur or Bull-man of Crete. The *Phaedo* is a playful recasting of this well-known myth. Socrates is the new, philosophic Theseus. He is the heroic savior of the friends gathered around Socrates as he is about to make his final journey — fourteen of whom are named. And their discussion of the soul and her fate, particularly in the final and most problematic stage of the argument, indeed resembles a logical labyrinth. Phaedo himself plays an important role as the fifteenth named member of the group around Socrates: He is the Ariadne whose narrative thread leads us into and through Plato's labyrinth of arguments.

But who or what plays the role of the Minotaur? From what, in other words, must Socrates' companions be saved? Is it their fear of death? Or is it the great evil known as misology or "hatred of arguments," the evil which, near the center of the dialogue, threatens to drown the conversation in disillusionment and despair? Or perhaps these are meant to be taken together — as the two "horns" of a dual-natured monster. This much is clear: The dialogue becomes ever richer as we try to think through the many points of contact between it and the myth it mimics. By the time we reach the very end of Phaedo's thread, we wonder: Is the Minotaur — whether as the fear of death or the hatred of argument — ever slain once and for all? Or, as its bullheadedness suggests, is it slain only to keep coming back to life again and again after each defeat?

Phaedo tells his story to Echecrates in Phlia, a city in the Peloponnese connected with the followers of Pythagoras. Indeed the spirit of Pythagoras, known to his disciples as *Autos*, hangs heavy over the *Phaedo*. The teaching that the body is the soul's prison is Pythagorean in origin, as is the transmigration of souls; and the notion of soul as a *harmonia* or tuning recalls the Pythagorean connection between ratios of whole numbers and musical intervals. But the Pythagorean theme closest to the heart of the dialogue is that of purification. Socrates returns to this theme often in the course of the discussion. The philosopher is depicted as the man who is, above all, pure and therefore free. The true philosopher, in Socrates' depiction, seeks to purify himself of all bodily entanglement in order to dwell with being or the forms. The *autos* language that pervades the dialogue is intimately bound up with this philosophic quest for purity.

But Socrates' relation to Pythagoreanism is problematic, to say the least. On the one hand, Socrates seems eager to form an alliance with the

Pythagorean devotion to purity, mathematics, musicality and health. On the other, Pythagoreanism, at least in its teaching that soul is a tuning, plays right into the hands of the Minotaur as the fear of death by implying that the soul is deathbound rather than deathless. The attack on soul-as-tuning is only one of several clues that the Pythagorean guise of the philosopher in the *Phaedo*, the ascetic depiction of philosophy as the practice of death and hatred of the body, is perhaps more caricature than characterization. If philosophy is hatred of the body, how do we account for the fact that Socrates at the age of seventy has a baby son (60A)? Or that, as Alcibiades tells us in the *Symposium*, Socrates, when pressed, always out-drinks everybody else, never gets drunk and seems to enjoy himself more than other people (220A)? Or that, as we discover in the *Phaedo*, Socrates enjoys playing with Phaedo's beautiful hair?

The *Phaedo* consists mostly of a conversation between Socrates and the two close friends, Simmias and Cebes, whose Pythagorean loyalties are both elicited and called into question throughout the dialogue. Their friendly twoness is played on in various ways as they wrestle with Socrates, with one another and with their fears and distrust. Simmias, although he occasionally expresses distrust, seems on the whole closer to trust, edification, musicality and right opinion. He agrees unquestioningly with Socrates' harsh depiction of the philosopher as a hater of the body and a practitioner of death. And it is Simmias who, late in the dialogue, is the prime recipient of the myth about the true earth. Cebes, by contrast, is the more logical and rigorously sceptical of the two. It is he who follows Socrates through the labyrinthine last argument. The differences between Simmias and Cebes cause us to reflect on the different and complex ways in which the human soul appears, and on how philosophic discussion, no less complex than the human soul, draws its sustenance and life from contrary but complementary sources.

The philosophic core of the *Phaedo* is usually thought to reside not in its drama but in the so-called "proofs for the immortality of the soul." Four such arguments are put forth in the dialogue: the argument from *contraries*, the argument from *recollection*, the argument from *invisibility* and the argument from *cause*.

These arguments present the reader with a variety of difficulties. The meanings of crucial terms shift from argument to argument. For instance, in some places the all-important term "soul" refers to the principle or cause of life, including plant life; in other places it clearly means intellect. Again, all the arguments are affected to some extent by Socrates' openly taken decision to "tell stories" or "sing incantations" on this his final day. The effects of this decision are particularly apparent at those points where "there" and "then," place and time, are readily attributed to souls and forms

— where, for instance, it is quickly concluded that forms constitute a region, albeit invisible, from which souls "came" or to which they will "go."

But perhaps the greatest difficulties stem from those "much-babbled-about" things, the forms. Three out of the four arguments rest on them, and they are readily accepted by both Simmias and Cebes. Can we afford to be so blithe? Even if we manage to persuade ourselves that not all talk about forms is mere babble and go along with Socrates' ruling hypothesis, difficulties remain, for the forms turn up in different guises in different arguments. Sometimes they appear as very distant objects of thought, unreachable in this body-ridden life. At other times, they turn up as features of our everyday experience, as, for instance, what we must be seeing whenever we note that equal sticks are not altogether equal. Or again, they show up right in front of us, engaged in mortal combat with their contraries whenever snow melts or numbers are added. Can these different "looks" be put together? No wonder Socrates both admits at one point that the argument is "still open to suspicions and counterattacks" and yet encourages Simmias and Cebes to "look into" and "sort out" their "first hypotheses" with greater care. In spite of the difficulties they present, indeed precisely because of those difficulties, Socrates' arguments — taken up in the right spirit, without the blindness of mere faith or the emptiness of mere scepticism — become a rich soil for questions and reflections of the most fundamental type.

The drama of the *Phaedo*, the drama in which the arguments just discussed have their philosophic life, may be playfully divided into fourteen parts, in imitation of the Twice Seven in the myth of Theseus. A brief synopsis of each part will give us both an overview of the whole and a thread of sorts through Plato's labyrinth.

I — Phaedo Himself [57A-59B]

Echecrates discovers that Phaedo himself was present on Socrates' last day and asks him to recount everything that was said and done. After telling Echecrates why Socrates' death was delayed (the embassy to Delos), Phaedo begins by speaking of the wondrous mix of pleasure and pain he experienced that day in the prison. It is with this mix of emotions that contrariety, so central to the entire dialogue, first comes on the scene.

II — Separateness and the Care of Death [59B-69E]

Phaedo begins the account proper by telling Echecrates the fourteen names of those he remembers to have been present. Plato, so Phaedo thinks, was ill and consequently absent. As the group of friends enters Socrates' cell, they come upon Socrates just released from his bonds. The pleasure he feels inspires him to reflect that Aesop would have done well to make up a story about pleasure and pain, about how the god settled their constant quarreling by tying their heads together.

Socrates' last conversation, as fabricated by Plato, does not begin as a conversation about the deathlessness of the soul. Indeed it looks at first as if Socrates himself might be inviting the group to discuss, not life and death, but the wondrous and Aesop-worthy relation between the two contraries, pleasure and pain. Phaedo had already expressed wonder at the mix of emotions in himself and in the group, and now Plato presents Socrates as echoing a similar experience. How, then, does the deathlessness of the soul come to be the central topic of Socrates' last conversation?

The mention of Aesop impels Cebes to ask about Socrates' own composi-tions, his musical settings of Aesop's fables and a hymn to Apollo. Evenus the poet-sophist wants to know, says Cebes, why Socrates has suddenly taken up composition. Socrates tells Cebes about his recurring dream and the di-vine exhortation to "make music." He ends by telling Cebes to tell Evenus that he, Evenus — "if he's soundminded" — should follow Socrates in death as soon as possible. This in turn leads to a discussion of why the philosopher, although a follower of death, will never take his own life. Even at this point, although the discussion turns in the direction of death, the question "Is the soul deathless?" is not yet explicitly raised. Instead the issue becomes: Is Socrates just in his willingness to abandon his friends and the gods? Simmias and Cebes bring charges against Socrates. They require Socrates to give an *apologia* or defense of why anyone who was truly wise would be as willing as Socrates seems to be, to get free of a good and divine master — of why Socrates is so willing to die. The analogy with Socrates' trial and the charges brought against him by Athens for impiety and corruption of the youth in-forms the entire conversation as it is related by Phaedo. Socrates is not only compelled to give an account in the theoretical sense: He must also give an account of *himself* before the court of Simmias and Cebes. He must seek to persuade them that the philosopher's calm acceptance of death is not a case of injustice against those who love him.

Here begins the emphatic denigration of the body that will continue throughout the dialogue. This denigration has an important rhetorical func-tion in regard to the charges of Simmias and Cebes. By denigrating the body and everything attached to body (including what we call "personal-ity"), Socrates is attempting to wean his two friends from the attachment to the man Socrates, whom they refuse to let die.

And so Socrates begins his defense. The true philosopher, he says, is "dead" to the body and its allurements, and philosophy is the practise of dying and being dead. The only good philosopher, it seems, is a "dead" philosopher. The body, we hear, is a kind of prison, from which the true philosopher seeks release. The philosopher strives for a precise and unerring vision of what *is*, and the body, with all its senses and emotions, is nothing but a continual nuisance and obstacle. As the effort to give oneself up to inquiry and therefore to free oneself from the body, philosophy is nothing less than "the care of death," a phrase Socrates uses at a later point. Since death is the release and therefore separation of the soul from the body, and since the philosopher, in all his inquiries, has always done nothing else than strive for such separateness and purity, it is only reasonable, argues Socrates, that the true philosopher will not make a fuss about death.

With this defense, Socrates proceeds to discuss wisdom or thoughtfulness as the highest and truest virtue and defines such virtue as a form of purification. He concludes his defense in a mythical mode by expressing the belief that There, in the Hades that awaits us all, he will dwell with gods and with "good comrades."

III — The Argument from Contraries [69E-72E]

The entire preceding defense of the true philosopher (which Socrates had conducted in a mysterious Orphic-Pythagorean mode and had attributed to "those who rightly philosophize") had been addressed to Simmias. Socrates' lofty tone and his concluding analogy between his defense before Simmias and Cebes and his defense before the Athenian judges, make it appear that Socrates was ready to "close his case." But Cebes speaks up and compels Socrates to talk some more. As Cebes points out, to argue that the philosopher should be cheerful in the face of death because There, in Hades, he will achieve the separation of soul from body that has been his practice and care throughout life, is to presuppose that the soul will still *be* once this separation has occurred. At this point, there begin the arguments for the deathlessness of the soul.

In turning the conversation to the proof of deathlessness, Cebes brings up two interrelated themes that will haunt the rest of the dialogue: fear of death and distrust. Cebes speaks for all human beings. He moves the conversation from the depiction and praise of the highest life of philosophy (Socrates' preceding Orphic defense) to life and death in general. It is Cebes who compels the conversation to take up the soul and her fate in relation to coming-to-be and passing-away, in a word, to process. It is because of Cebes, in other words, that the *Phaedo* combines a concern for the human soul with physics as the study of becoming as such.

Socrates rises to Cebes' challenge, or rather his probing anxiety, by appealing to the behavior of contraries. Echoing his earlier observation that pleasure and pain seem to evoke each other, Socrates puts forth the view that all contraries come into being from one another: the bigger from the littler, the worse from the better, the just from the unjust. He extends this view to include contrary processes like separating and combining, and cooling and heating. If indeed contrary processes or "becomings" always come in pairs, then the process of dying cannot fail to evoke its correlative process — returning to life. If the dead are generated out of the living, then the living must in turn be generated out of the dead. Becoming is a circle. And because of this circle, the soul — whose presence or absence marks a being as either alive or dead — must *be* before arriving in a body.

IV — The Argument from Recollection [72E-77A]

Cebes, recalling his earlier reminder about human distrust, tells Socrates that "we're not deceived in agreeing to these very things." He provocatively connects what Socrates has just put forth — Socrates' psychophysics — with the teaching that all learning is in fact recollection.

At this point, Simmias takes over the argument. He asks to be "reminded" of the demonstration of this teaching. Socrates obliges and goes through several examples, showing first that recollection can take place by means of associations other than similarity: The lover sees the beloved's lyre or cloak and recalls the beloved himself. Socrates then switches to recollection based on similarity. Plato leads us to wonder why recollection based on non-similarity, which Socrates provocatively connects with erotic experience, was brought up in the first place.

Earlier, in the high-flown defense addressed to Simmias, Socrates had first made reference to the forms with the designation, "each of the beings that's unadulterated and itself all by itself." In the argument from contraries, Socrates had in effect turned away from the forms to natural processes. With similarity-based recollection, the forms, again referred to as the "things themselves all by themselves," re-enter the conversation, this time as an integral part of a proof for the soul's deathlessness. Whereas recollection based on non-similarity was connected with erotic love, recollection based on similarity is connected with the sobriety of mathematics. Socrates uses the perplexing example of a "relational" form — the Equal. If equal sticks and stones indeed "remind" us of the Equal Itself by *falling short* of that Equal, and if we therefore had to have "seen" the Equal "beforehand" (that is, before we were embodied), then "our soul *is*, even before we were born." Simmias seems entirely convinced. He speaks of an "overwhelming necessity" to Socrates' argument, adding that "the account is taking refuge in a beautiful conclusion." But we are left with perplexities: Why does Socrates use, as his example of a form, a mathematical relation rather than a mathematical property of an individual thing (for example, an object's circularity)? And why *this* relation?

Many things are noteworthy about Socrates' treatment of recollection here. For instance, Socrates does not directly connect the recollection that "proves" the deathlessness of the soul with philosophic inquiry, as he does in the *Meno*, even though the arguments in both dialogues begin with mathematical discovery. The fact that Socrates does not here argue for deathlessness based on recollection as inquiry is perhaps due to the fear of Simmias and Cebes. Anxiety over the future, the fear about what happens to the soul *afterwards*, has usurped the place of philosophic *eros*, which tends, not onward and down, but *backward* and *up* to the truly deathless beings. This direction of inquiry is figured in the very word for recollection, *anamnesis*, the *ana* part of which means both "back" and "up." The fears of Simmias and Cebes, we might say, compel the argument to go "down" rather than "up." Socrates, who is unwilling to abandon them to their fears and who no doubt realizes that fear is an impediment to philosophic love, "descends" with them.

V — Songs for Children [77A-78B]

But has Cebes, that down-to-business fellow, been persuaded? Simmias comments on his friend's capacity for scepticism, calling Cebes "the mightiest of humans when it comes to distrusting arguments." He also suggests that he too is subject to "the fear of the many." What if the soul, he worries, were somehow put together at birth and then taken apart at death? Couldn't the circle of becoming then go on without the soul's continued existence? Cebes praises Simmias' perspicacity and remarks that only "half" the necessary argument has been given. Socrates reminds the two friends that the allegedly missing half of the argument has in fact already been taken care of. Nevertheless, he is willing to humor what he calls their "childish" fear of death. This lighthearted reprimand conveys a most important teaching: that one should not take the fear of death *too* seriously — if, that is, one's highest concern is with the pursuit of deathless being. Cebes, laughing, tells Socrates to go ahead: "Try to persuade us as if we were afraid." The little interlude ends with Socrates' telling the two friends that now, since Socrates is about to go away, they must search everywhere, even among "barbarians," for the "good singer" who knows how to charm away the bogeyman named Fear of Death.

VI — The Argument from Invisibility [78B-84B]

Socrates now gets down to business with Cebes. Together they explore the attributes of soul. If soul is found to be composite, then the old fear returns, for a composite soul could, and no doubt would, suffer decomposition into the parts or elements out of which she was made. A non-composite soul, on the contrary, would not suffer this. Socrates bases the inquiry on the distinction brought up earlier between the "beings themselves" and their sensuous participants. The former belong to the class of the unvarying and unseen, the latter to the class of the changing and visible. Soul is quickly found to be akin to being itself by virtue of her invisibility and natural hegemony over the body. She is "most similar to" the divine and deathless, while body is "most similar to" the human and the deathbound.

Socrates then reverts to his earlier mythical mode of speech. With a play on the word Hades — which closely resembles the Greek word for "unseen" — Socrates tells Cebes that the soul that has spent her days in philosophic purity, communing with being itself, goes off at the moment of death to a place like herself — "noble and pure and unseen." The play on "Hades" suggests that the philosopher, while alive in a mortal body, nevertheless, "goes to" a deathless "place" whenever he engages in philosophy. It suggests the here-unexplored possibility that the true Hades is not really an afterlife at all, that it is not "where you go next" but where you have the power to go *now*. To his happy portrayal of the philosopher, Socrates appends an ominous "likely story" about the fate of the impure, body-loving soul. He belabors his attack on body, telling Cebes that every pleasure and pain alike "nails the soul to the body." Socrates' rhetoric here seems intended to counter the fear of death with the fear of the basest enslavement. Socrates ends this section of the conversation by emphasizing to both Simmias and Cebes that death, for the pure or philosophical soul, is the escape from this enslavement and that the philosopher, if anyone, has no reason to fear death.

VII — The Lyre and the Weaver [84B-88C]

But Socrates' encouraging speech about not fearing death has an unsettling coda. He gives an all-too-familiar, all-too-vivid, depiction of just what we, in our childishness, fear: that our soul will be "scattered" and "blown away" at the moment of death, that she will "vanish and no longer *be* anywhere at all!"

The long silence that descends with Socrates' words envelops all present. Simmias and Cebes have a private interchange, but Socrates brings them out of hiding. He exhorts them strongly to voice their distrust. Then Socrates laughs and compares his "swan song" — his musical *logos* — to the song of real swans, who, he says, sing for joy on the day of their death. Simmias picks up the thread of the argument and speaks of the need for courage and resourcefulness. If a human being can't determine what's true, then, sailing upon human accounts as upon a raft, he must find among these accounts the one that's "best and least refutable." Simmias' speech foreshadows the "second sailing" we hear about later. It also summons the figure of Odysseus, that man of many ways, as a model for philosophic virtue. Odysseus is invoked at crucial moments in the *Phaedo*. He, Theseus, and also Heracles form a sort of heroic triumvirate in the dialogue. They provide a paradigm for Socrates' and his friends' efforts to slay the monstrous enemies of discourse.

Simmias voices his distrust through the image of a tuned lyre. If soul is to body as the tuning is to the lyre, then just as the tuning is destroyed along with the lyre, so too the soul is destroyed along with the body; for soul would be nothing more than this — "a blend of the elements of the body."

We then get to hear Cebes' distrust. He too uses an image. His objection is a more radical version of the one Simmias had put forth. Even if soul were "stronger and more long-lasting than body," even if she could outlive her body in the course of a great many deaths, what is to prevent the soul from eventually "wearing out?" It's like an old weaver-man, says Cebes, who wove and wore out many cloaks but wasn't "durable enough" to wear out all such cloaks for all time. Who knows, the soul's current "cloak" — Cebes here, or Simmias, or Socrates — may well be her last!

VIII — The Hatred of Argument [88C-91B]

At this perilous moment we approach the very center of the *Phaedo*, the heart of Plato's labyrinth. Echecrates irrupts into the conversation. He breaks in because Simmias and Cebes have just, each of them, made serious objections that threaten to undo Socrates' arguments. He wonders how he can trust any argument from now on. Back in Athens, Socrates has foreseen just this defeatism, and as if to speak to Echecrates from the grave, he turns to Phaedo, who will be telling Echecrates what happened next.

What follows is surely one of the most remarkable moments in the Platonic dialogues. Socrates plays with Phaedo's hair (something he did habitually, we are told) and guesses that tomorrow, when Socrates is no more, Phaedo will cut off those beautiful locks of his, adding that they both will have reason to cut their hair even today, "if the argument meets its end." This affectionate gesture is alone sufficient to dispel any notion that Socrates is simply a hater of bodily things.

Socrates calls on Phaedo to be his Heracles, as he will be Phaedo's Iolaus, in this exploit of saving the life of the account, incidentally illustrating what Phaedo has just told Echecrates: that he never admired Socrates more than on this occasion, because he was so kind and admiring in dealing with the young men's criticisms. For Heracles is the great hero and Iolaus his young companion, and Socrates is modestly proposing to reverse the proper roles. Now he warns of a danger, a certain experience they must guard against. To name it he coins a word on the analogy of "misanthropy," the hatred of human beings. It is "misology," the hatred of argument. Just as someone comes to distrust and hate all human beings because he has been repeatedly "burned" by an ill-placed trust, so a naive and artless way of trusting in arguments makes someone finally distrust and hate them all because no thing and no argument ever stays put, ever gratifies his demand for an argument that is deception-free. Then, instead of blaming his own ineptitude, he foreswears the activity of giving accounts and making arguments.

The remarkable drama that takes place between Socrates and Phaedo, so carefully placed at the center of the dialogue, suggests that the hatred of argument is more terrible than the fear of death, that this hatred is the true and deepest Minotaur in the soul. It also helps us understand the musical, incantatory function of Socrates' discourse — here, as elsewhere in the dialogue, no doubt connected with Orpheus' power of song. We hear on several occasions about the singer who can charm away the fear of death. That charm is perhaps no different from what we see actually going on in the drama before us, not just in the non-argumentative moments of the dialogue but also in the arguments themselves. The Cebes-like "business" in which philosophy ordinarily engages is possessed of a Simmias-like "music." The music of philosophic discourse calms the human anxiety about death, not by constructing irrefutable "proofs for the immortality of the soul," but by engaging the soul in the philosopher's everyday business of tending arguments.

IX — Tuning Undone [91B-95A]

Socrates now turns back to Simmias and Cebes. He helps them demolish the argument most familiar to them as disciples of Pythagoras, the argument that soul is a tuning, a mere relation of parts. Here begins the close-in fighting for the survival of reasonable speech and argument. Socrates briefly summarizes their respective forms of distrust and with that takes up the objection of Simmias. In his first "attack on Harmonia," he points out to Simmias and Cebes that the tuning-thesis doesn't "sing in accord" with the teaching that learning is recollection: If you trust the one, you've got to reject the other.

In his second assault, Socrates, now addressing himself to Simmias, argues that if the soul were a condition of tuning, and if being tuned always means being made orderly and good, then all souls would be orderly and good: Vice would be impossible. Not only that, but since one tuning can't be any more tuned or orderly than another, all souls would be equally virtuous.

The third and final attack appeals to the behavior of contraries. The crucial assumption here is that a tuning must always follow the disposition of its parts and never run contrary to them. If soul were indeed some sort of tuning, then since her parts would be the bodily elements in tension with each other, the soul could never run contrary to her body: The body would always lead. But this conclusion runs contrary to what had been agreed to earlier — that soul, by nature, rules. Socrates supports this view of soul's natural hegemony over the body by appealing to the countless occasions on which we restrain or check our bodily desires.

The attack on soul-as-tuning ends with an appeal to poetic authority. As the "Divine Poet" shows us, Odysseus (whom Simmias had indirectly invoked earlier in his image of the raft) speaks to his heart and controls himself. But the reference points to a difficulty that Socrates does not mention. Odysseus, in the passage from Homer, is controlling his anger and spiritedness rather than his bodily desires. He is in fact restraining himself from killing the maidservants for their having sacrificed all honor and loyalty to the pleasures of the body. If the soul is non-composite, and if the only opposition to be considered is that between soul and body, then how do we account for what seems to be a tension *within* the soul of Odysseus in Socrates' craftily chosen example?

X — The Threat of Blindness and the Second Sailing [95A-102A]

Socrates now turns to the objection of Cebes. Here he adopts a whole new strategy in order to make the argument, as he says, "more gentle." He pauses for a long time to consider something within himself — the very image of recollection. This pause is a signal that something very mysterious is coming; what they are searching for is "no trivial business," as Socrates says in the understated manner he habitually uses at crucial junctures, and it is indeed related to recollection. He shows them that what is at stake here is understanding "the cause of generation and destruction as a whole." *

---

* In turning to the difficulty raised by Cebes, Socrates suggests that they "come to close quarters in Homeric style." Throughout what follows we must recall that although Socrates now fights ostensibly for the deathlessness of the soul (which had been threatened by the images of lyre and weaver), he fights even more importantly for the renewed trust in the guiding power of philosophic arguments or *logoi*. The interlude with "Phaedo himself," in other words, had in effect displaced the fear of the soul's death with the fear that *all* arguments "die" in the end.

The epic, Homeric stature of what Socrates undertakes in the dialogue is not only signalled in the intimation that the stay-at-home Socrates has something in common with the widely travelled Odysseus, who "knew the mind" of many men, fought to save his comrades, and descended into Hades. It is also indicated in the Homeric allusion of the very first and the very last words of the *Phaedo*. When Echecrates opens with the words "You yourself, Phaedo — were you present on that day ... or did you hear from somebody else?", he is virtually quoting the question Odysseus is asked before he tells of his wanderings: "Were you yourself present or did you hear it from somebody else?" (*Odyssey* VIII 491). And Phaedo's final summation of Socrates, that he was "the best and, yes, the most thoughtful and the most just" of all others they had met, echoes what is said of old Nestor, that "he knew justice and thought beyond all others" (*Odyssey* III 244).

Socrates begins by giving Simmias and Cebes an insight into his intellectual development, in the course of which he is twice nearly brought to the very despair in reason that he has just so fervently denounced. When he was young, he was "wondrously desirous of that wisdom they call 'the inquiry into nature.'" At first, he would give the most ordinary answer to explain generation and growth: A human being grows by eating and drinking and adding flesh. But that was entirely unsatisfactory. Then he read a book by Anaxagoras, who said that Mind orders the world. He was delighted, until he saw that this "wise man" didn't actually use Mind in his causal explanations. Anaxagoras would, for instance, have said that Socrates was sitting in prison not because of any mindfulness but because his bones in their sockets were bent in a certain way. He would have neglected to show that it was Socrates' mind that judged it best for Socrates to endure the penalty imposed on him by the Athenians rather than to run off. Although Anaxagoras had asserted that Mind was the cause of all things, in the end he was just one more materialist. He could not explain why it was best for things to be as they are. Socrates here is like Odysseus, who is on the verge of his homecoming when an opened wind-bag blows him off course.

Socrates then tells Cebes that he had simply "had it" with looking into beings themselves and became afraid that he might become "soul-blinded." He sought refuge, as he puts it, in *logoi* or verbal accounts. Thus begins Socrates' famous "second sailing" in search of cause.

The passage about blindness and the refuge in *logoi* is one of the most difficult in the *Phaedo*. What exactly is the blindness Socrates fears? And what does *logos* refer to here? Socrates appears to be describing a conversion from the direct, intellectual perception of "things themselves" (presumably the head-on vision he sought in the physics of Anaxagoras), to the indirect but no less being-oriented activity of philosophic accounts based on the forms. The turn is not the conversion from "beings themselves" to images or likenesses of beings, as Socrates goes out of his way to make clear. Nor is the refuge in *logoi* the turn to the investigation of "language." Nor is *logos* here a "theory" or "concept," which would in effect displace philosophy's directedness to being with the directedness to the mere thinking of being and the invention of artificial structures. It appears to be the turn to a philosophic way of speaking that indeed "catches" the being of things, indirectly and therefore "safely," by attending to what speeches and things have in common — the genuine intelligibility of form, *eidos*, as opposed to the beguiling but sham intelligibility of process physics.

Socrates outlines a "method" of hypotheses, a way of inquiry that seems like an elaboration of the Odyssean raft Simmias had earlier described. These hypotheses, literally "puttings-under," are not hypotheses in the

modern sense of the term — rational, often mathematical conjectures intended to be verified by experiment — but rather sup-positions that support thinking and make speech possible. Speech here means all speech,
our ordinary everyday speech as well as account-giving and the arguments
in which Socrates has taken refuge. The first hypothesis is that there are
forms — the Beautiful Itself by Itself and many others — each of which is
itself a hypothesis. "Itself by Itself" is a kind of formula Socrates has de-
vised for these ultimate thinkables; it betokens the intensity of their being
and their independence from the variety of the things of sense that we call
by their name. Communion with these beings of thought is the intelligible
cause of both the coming to be and the abiding of the beings of sense. But
above all, the forms are responsible for our ability not only to name things
but also to engage in reasoned speech. Socrates makes it clear that he regards the hypothesis as a return, on a clarified plane, to his early inno-
cence, before he became discombobulated by the "wise," that is, sophisticated, causes given by those who inquire into nature. He calls his own way
simple, artless and naive. And he recommends it to Simmias and Cebes as
the way for all lovers of wisdom.

The rest of the dialogue up to the myth is devoted to showing how one
can think by means of hypotheses. The next part of the dialogue is thus,
aside from its matter, a demonstration for Simmias and Cebes, but even
more for us, of reasoning on the supposition of the forms.

XI — The Enthusiasm of Echecrates [102A]

Once again, Echecrates cannot contain himself. He breaks in a second
and last time, signalling that this central episode is over. It had consisted of
two complementary parts: a passionate defense of account-giving and a
particular way of doing it. Echecrates now voices his enthusiastic approval
of Simmias and Cebes for agreeing with Socrates on the right use of hypotheses. The slight interruption serves to remind us that the drama is not
strictly confined to Socrates' cell. By mediating between the actual events
and his listeners, Phaedo in his own way "brings the *logos* back to life." He
perpetuates it for Echecrates and his friends, just as Plato brings Socrates
back to life for us. Echecrates says outright what Plato surely intends us to
infer: that Socrates' way of hypothesis travels well and can be taken up
fruitfully in far off places and distant times.

XII — The Argument from Cause [102A-107B]

Phaedo picks up the thread of his narrative. At first Socrates talks with
Simmias, but soon Cebes enters and continues with Socrates to the very
end of this last section of the argument.

Here we reach the densest, most labyrinthine section of the dialogue. The basis for the entire discussion is the mutual exclusiveness of contraries, an exclusiveness that Socrates mythically (and somewhat comically) portrays in the language of combat and retreat. Socrates takes up the example of the Big and the Small. He argues that "the Bigness in us never abides the Small, nor is it willing to be exceeded." The Big and the Small are presented as at war with one another, like pleasure and pain in Socrates' much earlier reference to Aesop. The forms are possessed of inviolable identities, and this virginity makes a form inimical to its contrary. At the approach of its contrary, a form must either "flee" or "perish." An unnamed listener at this point speaks up and shows that he was paying close attention to the conversation and had been doing so all along. (Perhaps he is not one of the named fourteen because he doesn't need to be saved from inappropriate emotions and is simply "following the *logos*" with great interest.) He reminds Socrates that earlier it had been agreed that contraries, far from excluding one another, come to be out of one another. Socrates counters the objection by saying that the earlier assertion had not been about forms but about things. He then returns Cebes to the apparently indisputable claim that "a contrary will never be contrary to itself."

Socrates pursues the point by shifting to a new example: the Hot and the Cold and their influence over the behavior of fire and snow. Now the forms Hot and Cold behave as contraries usually do, according to what has been said so far. When one of them approaches, the other "either flees or perishes." But fire and snow, says Socrates, also behave in this way. When the Hot approaches snow, the snow that was once cold does not turn into snow that is now hot: It can either "move away" or else stay and perish *as snow*. Nor does fire "get cold" with the approach of snow. It too must either "get out of the way or perish."

Socrates then extends the argument to include the behavior of Odd and Even in relation to numbers. Why, we wonder, has Socrates chosen these examples in particular and this sequence? Do the examples, when taken separately and explored, point to the same or different conclusions? And do they tend to further the argument or undermine it? In any case, Socrates seems eager to draw a general conclusion: Contraries aren't the only thing not to admit one another — there are also those things that *contain* contraries.

At this point something unexpected happens. Socrates takes Cebes back to the very beginning of the argument and revises the earlier agreement about cause. He says he will now go beyond that first answer — the safe and unlearned one about the presence of a form. If somebody asks him, "What made this body hot?," Socrates will now say not "Hotness" but "fire." It is with this "fancier" or more sophisticated answer (an answer, we must note, that nevertheless continues to rely on the forms) that the argument —

questionably, to be sure — reaches its end. Socrates returns at last to the soul, now regarded as "that by which the body will be living." The reasoning embodied in the previous examples (Hot and Cold, Even and Odd) is now unquestioningly applied to soul in relation to body. Life and Death are contraries. Things that "contain contraries" behave the way contraries themselves do — they mutually exclude, and are inimical to, one another. But that which doesn't admit Death must be the deathless, and soul, since she brings Life to what she possesses, must "contain" the contrary of Death. Therefore, "soul is a deathless thing." Has this finally been sufficiently demonstrated? The usually sceptical Cebes seems to think so. He responds with an enthusiastic "Very adequately demonstrated indeed, Socrates." Socrates adds one more questionable condition to the argument — that the soul be shown to be imperishable or immune to decay as well as deathless. Cebes readily agrees that indeed the deathless must also be immune to decay. Socrates concludes: "So when Death comes at a man, his deathbound part, as is likely, dies, but his deathless part takes off and goes away safe and undecayed, getting out of Death's way." Socrates then returns to his earlier point, one of the constant refrains in his philosophic song: If the soul "takes off," then there must be some *place* she takes off *to*. That place is Hades — the Unseen.

Now that Cadmus has apparently been made "more gentle," Cebes says that he no longer has any distrust in the earlier arguments. He encourages Simmias "or anyone else" to speak up — while there's still time. Simmias too says he's no longer distrustful, "given what's been argued." But he qualifies his agreement with Cebes. He confesses to a lingering distrust based on the sheer magnitude of what they've been talking about and, by contrast, the weakness of human nature. Socrates responds by reinforcing this distrust while at the same time transforming it into a life-long task. He sobers up Simmias' vague anxieties about human infirmity by in effect telling Simmias to get down to work. Even our "first hypotheses," Socrates says, "must nevertheless be looked into more clearly." This presumably means, in particular, the hypothesis of the forms.

Earlier in the dialogue Socrates had invoked the figure of Penelope. There the true philosopher was *not* like Penelope, whose web was done only to be undone. He did not, once free of bodily entanglement, let his soul then fall shamelessly back into a liaison with body. But here, at the very end of the arguments in the *Phaedo*, Socrates both indirectly recalls and rehabilitates the figure of Penelope. The true philosopher is indeed like the wife of Odysseus. At the end of an argument, when a conclusion has been "woven," he must then go back to the beginning, separate the strands of which the argument is composed, and undo the web of *logos*. The *logos*, whose return to life the new Heracles has tried to bring about, is perpetuated precisely in this oscillation between weaving and unweaving. Argument goes on and is, in a sense, deathless — not just because valiant souls keep it up but because philosophic *logos* is itself inherently incomplete and never "meets its end."

XIII — The True Earth [107B-115A]

Socrates now turns away from argument, and from our trust and distrust in argument, to his myth about the true earth. Like the myths Socrates presents in other dialogues, this one has as its central point the extreme importance of taking care of our souls now in our mortal lives. The myth presents a genuine cosmos or beautifully ordered whole. In this it may be said to accomplish, however mythically, what the Mind of Anaxagoras could not. In place of the many earlier references to Hades, Socrates now presents an elaborate description of the shape and workings of the Whole. He combines the language of body-in-process, the language of physics, with an account of how various souls fare within this Whole.

According to Socrates' myth, the earth itself comes in three layers: the true earth, the hollows within it where we dwell (thinking we dwell on the surface), and the earth beneath us. The Earth Itself, round and pure and resplendent, remains at rest as a whole in the middle of the heavens. No pushes or pulls, no Atlas or air. No external force, in other words, is needed to keep it in place. The self-similarity of the heavens and the earth's own equilibrium suffice to keep it at rest. Life on the surface of the true earth mirrors this cosmic state of affairs. None of the tugs and pulls, none of the turmoil and violence that mark our life in the hollows is to be found there. True freedom, in other words, is the escape both from all process and from its attendant seriousness. The inhabitants of the surface of the true earth float free, dwelling in unconcealment, revelling in the sight of the things that *are*, like sight-seeing tourists on an eternal vacation. There are no faction-ridden cities, indeed no cities at all, on the surface of the true earth.

In the nether world, the world that lies below what we call earth, things are very different. Here force and constraint, turmoil and violence, characterize both the "look" of that world and the "lives" of those forced to stay there. Indeed the surgings and rushings of liquids under great pressure, the absence of light except in the presence of great heat, seem to mirror the inner turmoil of the most desperate of that world's inhabitants, who are in turn swept along, always at the mercy of someone or something other than themselves.

Yet for all its apparent chaos, the nether world turns out to have a structure. Not order and disorder but different principles of order make for the difference between above and below. The order of the lower world is the order of oscillation, of movement constrained or governed by and about a point, in this case the center of the earth. The center of the earth is also the center of a great tube that passes through the earth, the channel of Tartarus. This tube and its center together determine all fluid flow within the lower world. The *position* of Tartarus defines, in general, the path of flow, the meaning of "to" and "fro." The lower world is riddled by channels filled with everything from water to liquid fire, but every channel, however circuitous its path, must exit and sooner or later re-enter Tartarus. The center of Tartarus, in turn, defines the possible *extent* of flow: Just as a pendulum bob can never, over the course of its motion, end up at a point higher than its point of release, so too, liquid flowing out of Tartarus at one point can never re-enter it further from the center than the initial point of outflow.

Within this structure of ordered surgings, four rivers stand out along with Tartarus: Ocean ("Swift-flowing"), Acheron ("Distressing"), Pyriphlegethon ("Fire-blazing") and Cocytus ("Shrieking"). Here, too, a certain order is present — an order of contraries, as it were. Ocean and Acheron are paired with one another, as are Pyriphlegethon and Cocytus. They circulate in contrary directions and have their points of discharge "directly opposite" from one another, that is, at diametrically opposed positions on either side of the center. Moreover, Pyriphlegethon and Cocytus come nearest to one another when they pass by the Acherousian Lake. Those who have committed great but curable misdeeds spend most of their time in violent motion within Tartarus and are swept past the Acherousian Lake on the rivers only to ask forgiveness of those they harmed. In other words, this constellation of rivers seems to function as the moral center of the lower earth.

Where are *we* in this picture of the earth? The most beautiful things around us are mere fragments, yet fragments of the things above. Though our vision is clouded, we see the same heavens the surface-dwellers see. And some of the dappled beauty of their world comes from the mist and air around us, the "sediment" of the aether. Yet we seem to be equally connected to the earth below; indeed it is sometimes difficult to tell, in Socrates' account, where the hollows leave off and the underworld begins. That our Ocean's waters mix with and are governed by the same laws as their waters, that their Pyriphlegethon occasionally bursts forth in our world, are sufficient signs of the connection. Our own middling lives are suspended between these two extremes, and how we live now has everything to do with what region we will — or perhaps do — inhabit.

The myth, we must note, is addressed to Simmias, who, as has been said, seems to be the more lyrical and less dialectical. Socrates concludes his speech to Simmias with an exhortation. He speaks of the "noble risk" involved in taking the myth to heart, that is, not in believing all the mythical details, but in doing everything in life "so as to partake of virtue and thoughtfulness." Socrates again returns to that "good singer" who knows how to charm away the bogeyman, Fear of Death — but now the singer is *us*. We must take heart for our souls in the belief that the cosmos and the divine that lives within it are responsive to our quest for purification, especially the purification that is philosophy. Much of the *Phaedo* is about not what is absolutely and demonstrably true but about what the philosopher should tell himself — what, in a word, he should trust. Here Socrates reminds us that such trust in the goodness and order of the Whole is induced by philosophy as a form of music.

XIV — The End of Socrates [115A-118]

Socrates now says that he must "turn to the bath" and save the women the trouble of bathing a corpse — a gesture that combines care for his own purity with care for the sensibilities of others. At this point in the drama, Plato focuses our attention on the all-too-human Crito. Crito wants to cling to the man Socrates and to every precious minute and mortal concern that remains. Socrates attempts, gently but firmly, to bring Crito back to the extreme importance of what Socrates has always told them: to care for their souls by "walking in the footsteps" of what their conversations have shown them. Crito, however, quickly reverts to his care for Socrates' body: "But in what way shall we bury you?" Socrates at this point asks the others to "make a pledge" before Crito, to swear that Socrates will not remain behind at his death but will be "off and gone."

We now reach the concluding narration, in which Phaedo tells us how Socrates died. How does Plato's depiction of Socrates' final moments affect all that has been said up to this point? What exactly do we witness, and what can we conclude, as we watch the actual approach of Death?

If the accounts and arguments that Socrates has spent the day giving to and eliciting from his friends are more persuasive as examples and enactments of the way of life in which Socrates believes than as proofs of the survival of the soul after bodily death, then Socrates' demeanor in the hour and the moment of his death might matter even more than if he faced death utterly convinced that there was a life beyond. If he is really blithe even in his last moments on earth, we might suppose that he is a man who finds eternity in *this* life day by day, and who does not need to wait for physical death to die the philosopher's death, to turn away from the pleasures of the body to the delights of thinking. He might be a man who needs no special moment to live in the region of being — that is what his warmly human friend Crito does not quite understand.

But does that mean that Socrates is deceiving Simmias and Cebes, or even himself, when he sings them charms to banish the fear of death and when he casts himself as Theseus, their savior from the bull-headed monster, the

Minotaur? Not necessarily. Socrates recognizes that his young friends are frightened and that he has things to say to them that he himself may not need to hear. He is willing to enact a drama of conquered fear for their sake. If it is deception at all, it is also candor and kindness that makes him lead them through the labyrinth by the clue of his conversation to face — what?

After Socrates bathes, he sees his three sons and gives instructions to the women of his household. The servant of the Eleven arrives and bids a fond farewell to Socrates, calling him "the noblest and gentlest and best man among those who've ever arrived here." Socrates praises him for his noble tears and calls for the potion. Crito, with touching desperation, urges Socrates not to hurry — after all, there's still some sun on the mountains, still time to enjoy even the pleasures of sex before dying! Socrates then tells Crito that by acting as others do, he'd only be a laughingstock in his own eyes. He urges Crito: "Obey and don't act in any other way!"

When the potion-bearer arrives, Socrates treats him with all the respect due to one who has knowledge. He seeks advice on how to cooperate with the natural powers of the drug. Socrates at this point graciously takes the cup. Throughout the dialogue Socrates' glance has been emphasized. He looks at each speaker, keenly and attentively. Now near the end, when the man brings him the potion that is both a poison and a cure, he looks up at him from under his brows "with that bull's look that was so usual with him." A strange description, and it almost seems as if just at the stroke of death Socrates the Minotaur-slayer had himself turned into the Minotaur, whose death the young men have to watch so that they themselves may become monster-slayers. Socrates shows them the drama of the slaying of death so that they may see how harmless the monster is when approached in a safe and sure way.

We already know that Socrates has been judged by the potion-bearer not to be in an excited mood. For early on, he had warned Socrates not to engage in so much conversation as to become heated, because then a double dose of the poison would be needed to kill him. Now, when Socrates offers, in an enigmatic way, to use part of the potion to pour a libation to "somebody," it is clear that the man has judged that Socrates is calm and has brought only the minimum amount. So Socrates says that he must at least pray to the gods for an auspicious "emigration from here to There." And with that, he drinks.

All self-control breaks down at this point as the assembled friends seem to be devoured by yet another Minotaur — Grief. The whole company, including Phaedo, joins in the threnody of Apollodorus, who, throughout the entire conversation, had been weeping rather than following the argument. The music of discourse, it seems, has been utterly lost on him. Socrates rebukes them for their impious anti-music and exhorts them to propitious silence. Their shame restrains their tears. These tears, we must note, are not the noble tears of the servant of the Eleven, whom Socrates had praised. What, we wonder, is the difference between them? Why are the former ignoble and the latter noble? Perhaps it has something to do with the form as well as extent of the grief. Perhaps it is one thing to grieve but to accept the death of Socrates and another to grieve and not accept. This distinction fits with what the servant himself tells Socrates just before he leaves: "Farewell and try to bear these necessities as easily as possible." The servant is perhaps noble because, although he weeps, he does not do so uncontrollably: He is willing to say "Farewell!"

And now the approach of Death. In obedience to the potion-bearer, Socrates walks around until his legs are heavy and then lies down. Slowly Death comes upon him in the form of the Cold and the Stiff. It starts from below and works its way up: first the feet, then the legs, then the thighs. The potion-bearer calmly demonstrates the natural process by which Death operates. He tells the company that when the effect of the potion reaches the heart, Socrates then will be gone. Even as he says this, the parts of Socrates' lower belly grow cold.

Socrates now uncovers himself to make that last request Crito has been so eager to receive. "Crito," he says, "we owe a cock to Asclepius. So pay the debt and don't be careless." Some think that, since Asclepius is the god of medicine, Socrates is ordering a thank-offering (perhaps the one he was not allowed to pour himself) for being released from the disease of life. And that certainly fits with the fact that cocks were also sacrificed to the Egyptian god Anubis, identified with the Greek god Hermes, who guides souls to the underworld and by whom Socrates is fond of swearing. But why do "we" owe the thank-offering?

How we interpret the last words of Socrates, so redolent of the Theseus-theme of salvation, depends on what we think Socrates has been attempting to save his friends from, on who we think the real Minotaur of the *Phaedo* is. Certainly the fear of death is a prime candidate, and no doubt Socrates in his closing words expresses his gratitude to higher powers for his having been successful, at least on this occasion, in preventing his friends from being consumed by that fear. But as we have seen, at the center of Plato's labyrinth we find not the fear of death but the hatred of argument. Perhaps this is the deeper reason behind Socrates' thank-offering: On the day he died, surrounded by intensely anxious friends, he did indeed somehow manage to ward off the fear of death. But he did so not, as we have seen, by constructing irrefutable "proofs for the immortality of the soul," but by redirecting his friends' care to the renewed life of philosophic inquiry and discourse. Socrates thus dies bequeathing a task, not just to Simmias, but to all who know of Phaedo's account, when he says: "What you say is good, but also our very first hypotheses must nevertheless be looked into for greater surety."

Perhaps there is a second and harsher reason why Socrates himself, just before he drinks the potion, takes on the guise of the Minotaur. Perhaps there is something deadly even and especially about *him* — something from which, along with fear of death and hatred of argument, his friends need to be saved. Socrates in the *Phaedo* is surrounded by loving admirers who cannot bear to lose Socrates the man. The conversation begins, we recall, with Socrates' (to all appearances) blithe acceptance of death. This blitheness, stressed throughout the dialogue by Socrates' jokes and smiles, is taken hard by Simmias and Cebes, at least at first. In their indignation born of grief, they accuse Socrates of injustice to his friends. In effect, they cast him as a Theseus who saves his friends and fellow journeyers from all sorts of dangers only to abandon them in the end, as Theseus abandoned Ariadne on the isle of Naxos. Just before Socrates dies, it seems appropriate, then, that Socrates try to deliver his friends from the final Minotaur — their engrossing love of Socrates the man, a love that threatens to fill the soul with grief and indignation. He shows them the face that has the power to rivet attention on the man rather than on the speech and vision for which the man lived. The understandable fixation with Socrates the man is touchingly enacted in Crito's stubborn attentiveness to Socrates' body. This perhaps explains why Plato presents himself as absent on this momentous day. Unlike Apollodorus, Crito, Simmias and Cebes and all the others, Plato is not threatened by the most potentially seductive of all Minotaurs: He knows Socrates well enough to be willing to let the man Socrates die. Ironically, he is also the one who, in his dialogues, keeps Socrates perpetually alive for us readers — alive, enchanting and perhaps also *dangerous*.

Socrates then falls silent. After a little while, he makes a motion of some sort and is uncovered once more. He has composed his expression, and his mouth and eyes are open. They are closed by Crito.*

---

* We translate Phaedo's description of the last moment differently from others. The sense usually rendered is that when the attendant uncovered him, his eyes were fixed, and when Crito saw this he closed his mouth and eyes. The first word for eyes, *ommata*, also means visage or countenance; the second one, *ophthalmos*, means just the eyes. Moreover, the verb is active: It is Socrates who fixes, or better, composes his own features. Xenophon, in his *Defense of Socrates*, says that when Socrates had been condemned to death, "he went off blithe in countenance, demeanor and gait" (27).

There is a terrible case that seems almost the counterpart of Socrates' last moments: A man called Kirillov, in Dostoievsky's *Demons*, believes that he can prove his ultimate freedom by wilfully killing himself, but in the minutes before his self-annihilation he is seen to turn into a bellowing terrified beast, whose death disproves the claims of his life.

The course of Death has been knowingly plotted for us by the potion-bearer. We have watched its approach. But as for the moment itself, the arrival and very deed of Death — that remains cloaked in mystery, as does Socrates' final encounter. The final look of Socrates, however, while it may not tell us what Death is or even what Socrates experienced before he had "composed his expression," does offer a fitting, perhaps even comic, picture of what Socrates had lived for. In the open eyes and mouth, we have the very image of a man who devoted himself to vision and speech. If we put together the open eyes and mouth, we also have the gesture of wonder. The gesture seems to say, "So this is Death!", without, however, saying what Death Itself *is*.

Phaedo's narration ends, appropriately, with the praise of Socrates. If it is indeed the case that Socrates dies blithely and with welcoming wonder, a fact that has been noticed about Phaedo's last words in praise of Socrates begins to make sense. During his life, Socrates thought and talked about four particular virtues: wisdom, courage, moderation and justice. When Phaedo sums up Socrates' virtues, calling him the best, the most thoughtful and the justest of all men whom he and his friends had known, he leaves courage conspicuously unmentioned. Perhaps Plato is saying, through Phaedo, that a human being impassioned by the love of wisdom and absorbed in the search for being does not need courage in the face of death.

Was Socrates also the happiest of human beings? Phaedo does not say. And yet, we may infer from Socrates' lightheartedness, displayed throughout the dialogue, that Socrates died as he lived — neither indignant at misfortune and death, nor a passionless Stoic, nor, when all is said and done, a hater of the body who is glad to be relieved of the disease of life. He dies in full keeping with the conditions for happiness set out by Solon in Herodotus. He had served his city as soldier and gadfly and now dies in the fullness of old age (and with several sons), surrounded by a group of devoted friends. The condemnation of Athens even tends to ennoble him as a great man wrongly accused — a man who, on the day of his death, seemed to give ample proof of his belief in "good gods" and his scrupulous care for the souls of the young.

But the heart and soul of Socrates' happiness goes far beyond the temporal boundaries for happiness we find in Solon and Herodotus. This "higher" happiness lies in Socrates' pursuit of the divine and his devotion to speech and vision — a divine which, as the exact opposite of the divine in Herodotus, is not envious but rather opens itself up ungrudgingly, if perplexingly, to the exertions of inquiry. Throughout the *Phaedo* Socrates appeals to those deathless beings that the philosopher longs to "see" and "be with;" and throughout the *Phaedo* the singer Socrates, in an effort to deliver his friends from their tragic Muse, evinces a light and even comic mode. These two facts are connected. To give oneself to the love that is philosophy is to be liberated, above all, from tragedy and its deathbound Muse.

There is a story to the effect that Plato, after he met Socrates, went home and burned his tragic compositions. It was on that day that Plato slew at least one Minotaur and thus prepared to write a philosophic comedy entitled *Phaedo*. If Plato's readers are themselves delivered from their tragic-minded anxiety and are turned to the labors and the pleasures of philosophy, Plato himself might well have reason to say: "We owe a cock to Asclepius, reader. So pay the debt and don't be careless!"

Note

We have tried to adhere to the following translators' postulates: Our translation should be as faithful as possible to the Greek in vocabulary and in syntax. Plato's Greek makes sense, and so should our English. The dialogue is a lively conversation with frequent shifts in mood and diction, and our translation should attempt to convey that fact. The dialogue preserves the gestures and intonations of living language by means of dozens of those little parts of speech called "particles," and they should be rendered as accurately as possible by words or punctuation marks.

Capitals are used for terms referring to the forms and to classes, for example, "the Equal Itself," "the Visible," "the Odd" and "the Cold."

Italics are used for the verb *is* when this verb means "has being." Our italicized *is* thus renders what often appears in other translations as "exists."

For this translation we have used the Oxford text of John Burnet.

PHAEDO

Echecrates, Phaedo

57A   *Echecrates*: You yourself, Phaedo — were you present with Socrates on that day when he drank the potion in the prison, or did you hear from somebody else?

Phaedo: I myself, Echecrates.

Echecrates: Well, so what is it the man said before his death? And how did he meet his end? It'd be a pleasure for me to hear. For none of our fellow citizens from Phlia even visits Athens at all nowadays, nor has any stranger arrived from there in a long time

B   who could report anything sure to us about it — except, of course, that he drank the potion and died — but as for the rest, he was able to tell us nothing.

58A   *Phaedo*: Then you didn't even find out about the way the trial went?[1]

Echecrates: Yes, somebody did report that to us, and we kept wondering why, when the trial took place so long before, he apparently died so much later. So why was that, Phaedo?

Phaedo: A bit of chance came to his aid, Echecrates. For by chance the prow of the vessel that the Athenians send to Delos was crowned on the day before the trial.

Echecrates: Now what vessel's that?

Phaedo: This, as the Athenians say, is the vessel in which Theseus

B   once went off leading those Twice Seven to Crete, and both saved them and himself was saved.[2] So, it is said, the Athenians at that time made a vow to Apollo that if they were saved, an embassy

---

[1] Presentations of Socrates' trial for impiety and corruption of the young are to be found in Plato's *Apology* and Xenophon's work of the same name.

[2] For the significance of this myth, see Introduction, pp. 2-3. For the myth itself, see Plutarch's "Life of Theseus."

would be dispatched to Delos every year — which always and still now, from that year and every year, they send to the god.[3] Now once they've begun the embassy, it's their custom to keep the city pure during that time and to execute no one publicly until the vessel has arrived in Delos and come back here. And sometimes that takes a long time, when by chance the winds keep them

C back. The beginning of the embassy is the moment when the priest of Apollo crowns the prow of the vessel. And this happened by chance, as I say, on the day before the trial took place. For this reason Socrates spent a long time in prison, the time between the trial and his death.

Echecrates: Well, what were the circumstances of the death itself, Phaedo? What things were said and done? And which of the man's companions were present with him? Or did the officials not allow them to be present, so that he met his end bereft of friends?

D *Phaedo*: Not at all, but some were present, in fact many.

Echecrates: Well, put your heart into giving us as sure a report as you can about all these things, unless you happen not to be at leisure.

Phaedo: But I am at leisure, and I'll try to go through it for you. For to remember Socrates is ever the most pleasant of all things — at least for me — whether I myself do the speaking or listen to somebody else.

Echecrates: But, Phaedo, you'll certainly have for listeners others who are just like you. So try to go through everything as precisely as you can.

E *Phaedo*: For my part, wondrous were the things I experienced when I was present. For no pity overcame me, even though I was present at the death of a man who was my companion. For the man appeared to me to be happy, Echecrates, both in his manner and his words, so fearlessly and nobly did he meet his end; so that it came home to me that that fellow wasn't going to Hades without divine warrant, but would, if anybody ever did, do well

59A when he arrived There. For these reasons no pity at all overcame me, as would have seemed likely for one in the presence of sorrow. Nor again, was there pleasure in our being engaged as usual in philosophy — for our speech was in fact of this sort. Instead, as I realized deep down that very soon that man was about to

---

[3] Delos is an island in the Aegean Sea that contains a sanctuary of Apollo. Theseus is said to have stopped there for a dance of celebration on the way back from Crete.

meet his end, a simply absurd feeling was present in me, an unusual blend, blended together from pleasure and from pain too. And all who were present were pretty much in this condition, sometimes laughing, sometimes weeping, and one of us especially — Apollodorus. I suppose you know the man and the way he is.

B

Echecrates: Why, of course.

Phaedo: Well then, that fellow was utterly in this condition, and I myself was shaken up along with the others.

Echecrates: And who, Phaedo, happened to be present?

Phaedo: Among the locals, this Apollodorus was present, and also Critobulus and his father, and then there was Hermogenes and Epigenes and Aeschines and Antisthenes; Ctessipus the Paeanian was also there and Menexenus and some other locals. But Plato was sick, I think.

Echecrates: And were there any strangers present?

C

Phaedo: Yes, Simmias the Theban and Cebes and Phaedonides and, from Megara, Euclides and Terpsion.

Echecrates: What about this: Were Aristippus and Cleombrotus present?

Phaedo: Oh, no, they were said to be in Aegina.

Echecrates: Was anyone else present?

Phaedo: I think these were pretty much the ones who were present.

Echecrates: Well then, what do you say were the arguments?

D

Phaedo: I'll try to go through everything for you from the beginning. All throughout the days that preceded, I and the others had been in the habit of visiting Socrates, after gathering at dawn at the court in which the trial too had taken place — it was close to the prison. Each day we used to wait around, passing the time with one another, until the prison would open; for it didn't open early. And when it would open, we used to go in to be with Socrates and would mostly spend the whole day with him. Now on that day in particular we gathered even earlier. For on the day

E

before, when we came out of the prison in the evening, we found out that the vessel had arrived from Delos. So we passed the word to each other to come as early as possible to the usual place. And so we came, and the same doorkeeper who usually answered came out to us and told us to wait around, and not to go in until he himself told us to. "For the Eleven," he said, "are releasing

Socrates from his bonds and giving the word that he is to meet his end on this day."[4] We hadn't waited for a long time when he came and told us to go in. So we went in and caught Socrates just freed from his bonds and Xanthippe — you know her — holding his little boy and seated beside him. Now when Xanthippe saw us, she cried out and then said just the sort of thing women usually say: "Socrates, now's the last time your companions will talk to you and you to them!" And Socrates gave Crito a look and said: "Crito, have somebody take her home."

So some of Crito's people took that woman away, wailing and beating her breast, while Socrates sat up on the bed, bent his leg and gave it a good rub with his hand. And as he was rubbing it, he said: "How absurd a thing this seems to be, gentlemen, which human beings call 'pleasant!' How wondrously related it is by nature to its seeming contrary — the Painful — in that they're not both willing to be present with a human being at the same time; but if somebody chases the one and catches it, he's pretty much compelled always to catch the other one too, just as if the pair of them — although they're two — were fastened by one head! And it seems to me," he said, "that if Aesop had noticed this, he would've composed a story, telling how the god wanted to reconcile them in their war with each other, but when he wasn't able to do that, he fastened their heads together at the same point, and for that reason, when the one's present with somebody, its other follows along later. That's just how it seems in my own case too: After the Aching was in my leg from the bond, here comes the Pleasant, appearing to follow right after it."

Then Cebes broke in. "By Zeus, Socrates," he said, "you did well to remind me! In fact, some others have already been asking me about the poems you've made — the accounts of Aesop and the hymn to Apollo that you set to verse. And just the other day Evenus was asking what in the world you had in mind in making these verses after you came here, when before this you never made any at all.[5] So if you care about my being able to answer Evenus the next time he asks me — and I know for sure that he will ask — tell me what I should say."

"Then tell him the truth, Cebes," he said, "that I didn't make these verses because I wanted to rival that fellow, or his poems,

---

[4] The Eleven were the officials in charge of prisons and executions.

[5] Evenus, who was visiting Athens from Paros at the time of Socrates' trial, was both a sophist, that is, a paid teacher of virtue, and a poet. He is mentioned by Socrates in the *Apology* (20B).

in artistry — I knew *that* wouldn't be easy — but to test what certain dreams of mine might be saying and to acquit myself of any impiety, just in case they might be repeatedly commanding me to make this music. Here's how they went: The same dream visited me often in my past life, appearing sometimes in one aspect and sometimes in another but always saying the same thing. 'Socrates,' it said, 'make music and work at it!' Now at

61A least in former times, I assumed that it was exhorting me and urging me on repeatedly to the very thing I was doing, and that just as people encourage runners, the dream kept urging me on to do what I was doing — to make music — since philosophy, in my view, is the greatest music and that's just what I was doing. But now, once the trial had taken place and while the festival of the god prevented me from dying, it seemed that if the dream had indeed often ordered me to make this popular music, I shouldn't disobey but should make it; for it seemed safer not to

B   go away before acquitting myself of any impiety by making poems and obeying the dream. So first I made a poem to the god whose day of sacrifice was at hand. And taking note that a poet, if he's to be a poet, has to make stories, not arguments, and that I myself was not a storyteller, therefore after the god I turned to the stories of Aesop, the ones I had at hand and knew — whichever I chanced on first — and made them into poetry. So tell Evenus this, Cebes, and bid him farewell, and tell him, if he's

C   soundminded, to follow me as quickly as possible. I'm going away, as it seems, today — for the Athenians so order it."

And Simmias said, "How can you exhort Evenus in this way, Socrates? By now I've met the man often. It's pretty certain, from what I've perceived, that he won't be willing to be persuaded by you in any way whatsoever."

"What!" said he. "Isn't Evenus a philosopher?"

"To me at least he seems to be one," said Simmias.

"Well then, Evenus and everybody who takes a worthy part in this business will be willing to take my advice. Though perhaps he won't do violence to himself — they say it isn't lawful."

D   And with these words, he put his feet down on the earth and for the rest of the time conversed sitting in this way.

Then Cebes asked him, "What are you saying, Socrates: It isn't lawful for him to do violence to himself, but the philosopher should be willing to follow after somebody who's dying?"

"What, Cebes! Haven't both you and Simmias heard about

such things, you who've spent time with Philolaus?"

"At any rate, nothing sure, Socrates."

E "Now certainly I too speak of them only from hearsay. What I happen to have heard, however, I don't begrudge telling. For perhaps it's especially fitting for somebody who's about to emigrate to that place to examine and also to tell stories about the emigration There — what sort of thing we think it is. For what else would one do in the time until the setting of the sun?"

"On whatever grounds, then, do they say that it's not lawful for somebody to kill himself, Socrates? For I've already heard Philolaus too, when he was staying among us, say what you said just now, and I've heard it from some others as well: 'One must not do this.' But I've never heard anything sure about these things from anyone."

62A "But you should take heart," he said, "— maybe you'll hear something. And yet, it will perhaps appear wondrous to you, if this case alone among all the others is simple — if it never turns out for humankind, as it does in other cases, that sometimes and for some men it's better to be dead than alive, and in the case of these human beings for whom it's better to be dead, perhaps it appears wondrous to you that it isn't pious for them to do themselves good, but instead they must wait around for another benefactor."

And Cebes, with a gentle laugh, said, "Doan Zeus knowet!," speaking in his own dialect.

B "For it would seem," said Socrates, "to be unaccountable if put this way. And yet just maybe it does have an account. The account that's given about these things in the Mysteries — that we humans are in a sort of garrison and one is bound not to release oneself from it nor to run off — appears to me to be a grand one and not easy to make out. And yet this, at any rate, seems to me to be well put, Cebes: The gods care for us, and we humans are one of the gods' possessions. Or doesn't it seem so to you?"

"To me it does," said Cebes.

C "Now if one of your possessions were to kill itself, when you didn't signal that you wished it to die," he said, "wouldn't you be harsh with it, and if you had some means of punishing it, wouldn't you?"

"Of course," he said.

"Well then, perhaps in this way it's not unaccountable that a man's bound not to kill himself before god sends some necessity — like the one that's now upon us."

"At least that appears likely," said Cebes. "And yet, what you D   were saying just now, that the philosophers would be ready and willing to die, seems like an absurdity, Socrates — if in fact what we were now saying is reasonable, that god is our caretaker and we are his possessions. For it's not reasonable for the most thoughtful men not to make a fuss when they leave behind this position of service, in which the very best overseers there are, the gods, watch over them. For at least the thoughtful man does not, I suppose, imagine that he'll take better care of himself once he's become free. But a mindless human being would perhaps imag- E   ine that one must flee from one's master. He wouldn't reason that one must not flee from one's master — at least a good one — but all the more remain with him, and hence he'd flee irrationally. But the mindful man would, I suppose, always desire to be with somebody better than himself. And yet, put this way, the con- trary of what was said just now is likely — that it's fitting for the thoughtful to make a fuss when they die and for the thoughtless to rejoice."

When Socrates heard this, it seemed to me he was pleased 63A   with Cebes' down-to-business manner. And he glanced at us and said, "Boy, that Cebes is always tracking down some argument or other and isn't at all willing to be persuaded right off by what anybody says!"

And Simmias said, "Well, Socrates, right now I myself also think there's something to what Cebes is saying. For why would men who are truly wise want to flee from masters who are their betters and readily get free of them? And I think Cebes is aiming his argument at you, because you're so ready to abandon us and the gods, who, as you yourself agree, are good rulers."

B   "What you say is just," he said, "for I think what you're both saying is that I should make my defense against these charges, just as in the law court."

"Certainly," said Simmias.

"Well then," said he, "I'd better try to give a more persuasive defense before you than I did before my judges. For if I didn't think, Simmias and Cebes," he said, "that I was going to come, first of all, among other gods who are wise and good, and sec- ondly among human beings who've met their end and are better C   than those here, I would've done injustice not to make a fuss about death. But as it is now, know well that I hope to arrive among good men. I wouldn't altogether insist on this; nevertheless, if there were any such thing I would insist on, know that it'd be this — that I was going to come among gods who are completely good masters. So for these reasons, not only am I not making a fuss, but I have high hopes that there's something for those who've met their end, and just as it's been said of old, something far better for the good than for the bad."

"So then, Socrates," said Simmias, "are you of a mind to go off and keep this thought to yourself, or would you give us a share of it too? To me at least this good surely seems to be a common one that belongs to us as well; and at the same time it will be your defense — if, that is, you persuade us by what you say."

D

"That's just what I'll try to do," he said. "But first let's look into what Crito here wants. Seems to me he's been wanting to say something for a long time now."

"What else but this, Socrates," said Crito, "that for a long time now the fellow who's to give you the potion has been telling me that I should warn you to converse as little as possible? He says people who do a lot of conversing get all heated up and that one mustn't interfere in any such way with the potion. He says if that does happen, sometimes those who do this sort of thing must be compelled to drink it twice and even three times."

E

And Socrates said, "Let him be! Just have him prepare his potion and be ready to give it twice and, if he must, even three times."

"I pretty much knew you'd say that," said Crito, "but he's been giving me trouble for a long time now."

"Let him be!" he said. "But now I want to render my account to you my judges, to tell you why it appears reasonable to me that a man who's genuinely spent his life in philosophy is confident when he's about to die and has high hopes that when he's met his end, he'll win the greatest goods There. Just how all this could be so, Simmias and Cebes, I shall try to tell you.

64A

"Others are apt to be unaware that those who happen to have gotten in touch with philosophy in the right way devote themselves to nothing else but dying and being dead. Now if this is true, surely it would be absurd if they put their heart into nothing but this all their life, and then, when it comes, they make a fuss about the very thing to which they had long given both their hearts and their devotion."

B   And Simmias said with a laugh, "By Zeus, Socrates, right now I'm not much for laughing, but you did make me laugh! For I think that the many, if they heard this very thing, would be of the opinion that you spoke all too well about those who philosophize. And the people back home would entirely agree with them that those who philosophize are genuinely ripe for death, and indeed they're not unaware that they deserve this plight."

"And they'd be speaking the truth, Simmias, except of course about their not being unaware. For they're unaware of this: in what way those who truly are philosophers are ripe for death and in what way they are worthy of death and of what sort of

C   death. Let us then," he said, "talk amongst ourselves and bid those others farewell. Do we consider that there's such a thing as death?"

"Of course," said Simmias, breaking in.

"And is it anything but the freeing of the soul from the body? And is this what it means to have died: for the body to have become separate, once it's freed from the soul and is itself all by itself, and for the soul to be separate, once she's freed from the body and is herself all by herself? Death couldn't be anything other than this — could it?"

"No, just that," he said.

"Now, my good man, see if your opinion is just the same as

D   mine. For I think we'll know more about what we're looking into by beginning with this: Does it appear to you that being serious about the so-called pleasures, such as those of food and drink, goes with being a philosophical man?"

"Least of all, Socrates," said Simmias.

"And what about the pleasures of love-making?"

"No way."

"And what about any other servicings of the body? Does such a man seem to you to regard any of them as worthy of honor? For instance, there's the attainment of diverse cloaks and sandals and the other, body-related beautifications. Does he seem to you to

E   honor them? Or does he hold them in dishonor, except insofar as there's an urgent necessity for him to have his share of them?"

"Seems to me he holds them in dishonor," he said, "at least the one who's truly a philosopher."

"All in all, doesn't it seem to you," he said, "that the business of such a man is not with the body; instead, he stands apart from it and keeps turned toward the soul as much as he can?"

"Seems so to me."

65A   "First then, in such matters, isn't the philosopher clearly beyond other human beings in releasing the soul from communion with the body as much as possible?"

"Apparently."

"And certainly, Simmias, most human beings are of the opinion that the man for whom none of these things is pleasant and who doesn't have a share of them doesn't deserve to live. In fact, the man who thinks nothing of the pleasures that come through the body is pretty much headed for death."

"What you say is certainly true."

"And what about the very attainment of thoughtfulness? Is
B   the body an impediment or not when somebody takes it along as a companion in his search? Here's the sort of thing I mean. Do sight and hearing possess any truth for human beings, or is it the case that we neither hear nor see anything precise — the sort of thing even the poets are always babbling about to us? And yet, if among the bodily senses seeing and hearing are neither precise nor clear, the rest scarcely are, for, I suppose, these are all inferior. Or don't they seem so to you?"

"Certainly," he said.

"So when," said he, "does the soul get in touch with truth? For when she attempts to look at something along with the body, it's clear that then she's deceived by it."

C   "What you say is true."

"Then isn't it in her act of reasoning, if anywhere, that something of the things that *are* becomes very clear to her?"

"Yes."

"And I suppose the soul reasons most beautifully when none of these things gives her pain — neither hearing nor sight, nor grief nor any pleasure — when instead, bidding farewell to the body, she comes to be herself all by herself as much as possible and when, doing everything she can to avoid communing with or even being in touch with the body, she strives for what *is*."

"That's so."

D   "Then here too, doesn't the soul of the philosopher especially hold the body in dishonor and flee it and seek to become a soul herself all by herself?"

"Apparently."

"And what about this sort of thing, Simmias: Do we claim that there is some Just Itself — or no such thing?"

"We do claim it, by Zeus!"

"And also some Beautiful and Good?"

"Why, certainly."

"Well, ever see anything of that sort with your eyes?"

"In no way," said he.

E "But did you lay hold of them by any other sense that comes through the body? And I'm speaking about the Being of all such things, about Bigness and Health and Strength and, in a word, all the rest — whatever each happens to be. Is what's truest about them beheld through the body? Or does it work this way: He among us who best prepares himself to think through most precisely each thing he investigates — that man would come closest to recognizing each thing?"

"Certainly."

66A "Then wouldn't that man do this most purely who approaches each thing as far as possible with thought itself, and who neither puts any sight into his thinking nor drags in any other sense along with his reasoning; but instead, using unadulterated thought itself all by itself, he attempts to hunt down each of the beings that's unadulterated and itself all by itself, and once he's freed himself as far as possible from eyes and ears and, so to speak, from his whole body, because it shakes the soul up and doesn't let her attain truth and thoughtfulness when the body communes with her — isn't this the man, Simmias, if anyone, who will hit upon what *is*?"

"Extraordinary how truly you speak, Socrates!" said Simmias.

B "Therefore it's a necessity," he said, "that for all these reasons the true-born philosophers would be won over to some such opinion as this and so would say something like the following to one another: 'It looks like there's a shortcut that brings us to this conclusion — that as long as we have the body accompanying the argument in our investigation, and our soul is smushed together with this sort of evil, we'll never, ever sufficiently attain what we desire. And this, we affirm, is the truth. For the body deprives us of leisure on thousands of occasions through the ne-

C cessity for food. And what's more, when it comes down with certain diseases, these get in the way of our hunt for what *is*. And it fills us up with erotic loves and with desires and terrors and all manner of images and lots of nonsense, so that because of the body it becomes truly and genuinely impossible, as the saying goes, for us to be thoughtful about anything at all *ever*! After all, nothing other than the body and its desires produce wars and factions and battles; for all wars come about for the sake of get-

D ting money, and we're compelled to get money for the sake of the body, to whose service we're enslaved. And so, on account of this — the body — and for all these reasons, we have no leisure for philosophy. And the worst of it all is that if a bit of leisure does come along for us and we get away from the body and turn to investigating something, the body constantly turns up again and makes noise and trouble in our searchings and drives us crazy, so that because of it we're incapable of seeing the truth — and this is

E where it's really pointed out to us that if we're ever going to know anything purely, we've got to free ourselves from the body and behold things themselves with the soul herself. And then, as it seems, the thoughtfulness we desire and whose lovers we claim to be will be ours — when we've met our end and, as the argument shows, not while we're alive. For if it isn't possible to recognize anything at all purely when in company with the body, one of two things must follow. Either there's nowhere to attain know-

67A ing, or else it's only for those who've met their end — for then the soul will be herself all by herself separate from the body — but not before. And in the time we're alive here's how we'll come closest, it seems, to knowing: if as much as possible we in no way consort with the body or commune with it — unless it's an absolute necessity — or fill ourselves up with its nature, but purify ourselves from it until the god himself shall release us. And when, in this way, we are pure and free of the thoughtlessness of the body, we shall, as is likely, be in the company of things that are

B pure as well and, through our own selves, shall recognize everything unadulterated — and this, no doubt, is the True. For it isn't at all lawful that the not-pure should touch the pure.' That's the sort of thing, Simmias, all who rightly love learning will, I think, necessarily say to each other and hold as an opinion. Or doesn't it seem so to you?"

"More than anything, Socrates."

"Then," said Socrates, "if these things are true, my comrade, there's great hope that when I arrive at the end of my journey, There — if indeed anywhere — I shall sufficiently attain what

C our constant business in our bygone life has been for. And that's why the emigration which has now been imposed on me is begun in good hope, and so it is for any other man who considers that his thinking has been prepared by being, as it were, purified."

"Certainly," said Simmias.

"And purification — doesn't it turn out to be this, as was said way back in the argument: Isn't it separating the soul from the body as much as possible and habituating her to gather and collect herself all by herself out of all the sites of the body and to dwell as much as possible, both in the present and in the time to come, alone by herself, released from out of the body just as from

D   bonds?"

"Certainly," he said.

"Isn't this what goes by the name of death — the release and separation of soul from body?"

"Altogether so," said he.

"And releasing her, as we claim, is what those and only those who philosophize rightly are always putting their heart into most of all, and this very thing is the care of the philosophers: the release and separation of soul from body. Isn't it?"

"Apparently."

"Then wouldn't it be laughable, as I was saying in the begin-

E   ning, for a man who'd been preparing himself in life to live as close as possible to being dead to make a fuss when death finally came to him?"

"Why, certainly it's laughable."

"In fact, Simmias," he said, "those who philosophize rightly make dying their care, and of human beings to them least of all is being dead terrifying. And look at it on these grounds: If they'd been at odds with the body in every way and desire to keep the soul herself all by herself, wouldn't it be great unreason if they were terrified and made a fuss when this happened, and weren't

68A   pleased to go There, where there was hope for those who'd arrived to get what they've been in love with throughout life — and they were in love with thoughtfulness — and to be free of the company of that with which they'd been at odds? Again, many people have been willing to pursue their human loves to Hades when they've died — their boyfriends, wives and sons — led by the hope that they'll see and be together There with those they desired. Then will the man who's genuinely in love with thought-

B   fulness and who's taken a firm hold of this same hope that nowhere else but in Hades will he encounter it in a manner worth speaking of, make a fuss about dying and not be pleased to go There? We must suppose this is so, my comrade, whenever somebody's a genuine philosopher. For this will definitely be his opinion: He'll encounter thoughtfulness purely nowhere but There. If this is how things stand, wouldn't it be great unreason, as I was just saying, if such a man should be terrified at death?"

"Very great, by Zeus!" said he.

C "Then," he said, "this is sufficient proof for you that any man you see making a fuss at the prospect of dying was not a lover of wisdom but a lover of the body. And I suppose this same man turns out to be a lover of money and a lover of honor, of either one of them or of both."

"It's certainly as you say," he said.

"Then isn't it the case, Simmias, that what goes by the name of courage especially befits those in this condition?"

men of wisdom or body?

"In every way," he said.

"Then also, the moderation that even the many name moderation — not being all aflutter about desires but making little of them and being orderly — doesn't that befit these men alone, men who especially make little of the body and live their lives in philosophy?"

D "It's a necessity," he said.

"For if you're willing," said he, "to take note of the courage as well as the moderation of other men, it'll seem to you to be absurd."

never mind

"How so, Socrates?"

"You know," said he, "that all other men regard death as among the great evils?"

"Very much so," he said.

"Then don't the courageous among them, whenever they face death, face it through terror at greater evils?"

"That's so."

"Therefore all but the philosophers are courageous by fearing and by fear. And yet it's certainly unreasonable for somebody to be courageous by fear and cowardice."

E "Certainly."

"And what about the orderly ones among them? Aren't they affected in this same way — they're moderate by a sort of self-

indulgence? To be sure, we say this is impossible, but nevertheless what characterizes this simple-minded moderation turns out
for them to be like that. For since they're terrified of being robbed
of some pleasures and yet desire them, they keep away from some
through being mastered by others. And yet they call being ruled
69A   by pleasures self-indulgence. Nevertheless, as it turns out, they
master some pleasures only because they're mastered by other
pleasures. And this is similar to what I was saying just now, that
they've been, after a fashion, moderated by self-indulgence."

"So it seems."

"Bless you, Simmias, maybe this isn't the right way of making exchanges for virtue, by exchanging pleasures for pleasures
and pains for pains and terror for terror and the greater for the
less, as if they were coins; but maybe this alone is the right coin
for virtue, the coin for which all things must be exchanged —
B   thoughtfulness. Maybe this is the genuine coin for which and with
which all things must be bought and sold; and maybe courage
and moderation and justice and true virtue as a whole are only
when accompanied by thoughtfulness, regardless of whether pleasures and terrors and all other such things are added or subtracted.
But when such things are separated from thoughtfulness and are
exchanged one for the other, maybe such virtue isn't anything
but a kind of shadow-painting and is genuinely suited only for
slaves and has nothing in it either healthy or true; but maybe the
C   true and genuine virtue is a sort of purification from all these
things, and maybe moderation and justice and courage and
thoughtfulness itself are nothing but a kind of purifier. And it
looks as if these people who instituted our mystic rites weren't a
bunch of bunglers but spoke with a genuine hidden meaning
when they said long ago that whoever arrives in Hades ignorant
of the mysteries and uninitiated will lie in Muck, but that he who
D   arrives There purified and initiated will dwell with gods. For as
they say about the mysteries: 'Many the wand-bearers, but the
celebrants few.' And these celebrants are in my opinion none other
than those who've philosophized rightly. Now I too, as one of
them, have left nothing undone in my life that was in my power,
but have put my heart into becoming one of them in every way.
But whether I've put my heart into it rightly and whether we've
accomplished anything, we shall know for sure, as it seems to
me, only when we've gone There — I in just a little while, if god
is willing. So then, Simmias and Cebes," he said, "that's my de-
E   fense of why it's reasonable for me to leave you and the masters

I've got here without taking it hard or making a fuss: because I believe that There too, no less than here, I shall meet up with good masters and good comrades as well. If I've been at all more persuasive to you in my defense than I was to the Athenian judges, it would be well."

Now when Socrates had said all this, Cebes broke in and said: "Socrates, the rest seems to me to have been beautifully put, but what you said about the soul induces a lot of distrust in human beings. They fear that the soul, once she's free of the body, is no longer anywhere and is destroyed and perishes on that very day when a human being dies; and that as soon as she's free of the body and departs, then, scattered like breath or smoke, she goes fluttering off and is no longer anywhere. Of course, if she should *be* somewhere, herself all by herself, collected together and freed from those evils you went through just now, there'd be a great hope — a beautiful hope — that what you say, Socrates, is true. But this point — that the soul *is* when the human being dies and holds onto both some power and thoughtfulness — probably stands in need of more than a little persuasive talk and assurance."

"What you say is true, Cebes," said Socrates, "but now what should we do? Or do you want us to tell a more thorough story about these things to see whether what we're saying is likely or not?"

"For my part," said Cebes, "it'd be a pleasure to hear whatever opinion you have about them."

"I can't imagine then," said Socrates, "that anyone hearing us now, even if he were a comic poet, would say that I jabber and make speeches about matters that aren't my business.[6] So if you're of this opinion, we should investigate the matter thoroughly.

"And let's investigate it in some such way as this: Either the souls of human beings who've met their end are in Hades or they're not. Now there's a certain ancient account, one that we hold in memory, that souls *are* There having arrived from here, and that they arrive here again and come to be from the dead. And if this is so, and the living come to be again out of those who've died, could anything else be the case but that our souls *are* There? If they weren't somewhere, they couldn't come to be

---

[6] Socrates turns up in Aristophanes' comedy *The Clouds* as the proprietor of a "thinkery," where, suspended in a basket, he teaches his pupils to worship clouds and to make the worse arguments seem the better. Socrates had alluded to this play in his trial in the *Apology*.

again; and it'd be sufficient proof that this is so, if it should in fact become clear that the living come to be from nowhere else but from the dead. But if this isn't so, we'd need another account."

"Certainly," said Cebes.

"Now if you want to understand this more easily, don't look only to human beings," said he, "but also to all animals and plants. And in sum, let's take a look at all things that have a becoming — whether they all, as contraries, come to be from anywhere else but from their contraries, at least those that happen to have some such contrary; for example, what's beautiful is contrary to what's ugly, I suppose, and what's just to what's unjust, and surely thousands of other things are like that. So let's investigate whether it's necessary for whatever has some contrary to come to be from nowhere else but from its own contrary. For example, whenever something comes to be bigger, isn't it a necessity that it become bigger later from something that was littler before?"

"Yes."

71A   "And also if something comes to be littler, won't it come to be littler later from something that was bigger before?"

"That's so," he said.

"And further, the weaker comes from the stronger, and the quicker from the slower?"

"Of course."

"What about this: If something comes to be worse, doesn't it come from what's better, and if more just, from what's more unjust?"

"Certainly."

"Well then," he said, "do we have the matter well enough in hand: All contrary things come to be in this way — from contraries?"

"Of course."

"And again, what about this: Aren't there, in the case of all
B   contraries, since they come in pairs, something like two becomings between them, from one to the other, and, again, from the other back to the first — between a bigger and a littler thing isn't there growth and decay, and so we call the one 'growing' and the other 'decaying'?"

"Yes," he said.

"And separating and combining and cooling and heating and

likewise everything else — even if here and there we don't make use of names — isn't it in fact everywhere necessary that they come to be from one another and that there's a becoming from each member of the pair to the other?"

"Certainly," said he.

C   "Well then," he said, "is there some contrary to being alive, as being asleep is to being awake?"

"Certainly," he said.

"What?"

"Being dead," he said.

"Then don't these come to be from one another, if in fact they are contraries; and because they are two, aren't there two becomings between them?"

"Why, of course."

"Well then," Socrates said, "I'll tell you one of the yoked pairs that I was speaking about just now — both it and its becomings — and you'll tell me the other. I say there's being asleep and being awake, and that being awake comes to be from being asleep and being asleep from being awake, and the becomings that go with these two are falling asleep and waking up. Is that sufficient for you," he said, "or not?"

D

"Certainly."

"Now you," he said, "speak to me in just this way about life and death. Don't you say that being dead is contrary to being alive?"

"I do."

"And they come to be from one another?"

"Yes."

"Then what's the thing that comes to be from the living thing?"

"The dead thing," he said.

"And what," said he, "from the dead one?"

"It's necessary to agree," he said, "the living thing."

"Therefore, Cebes, living things — living people too — come to be from the dead?"

E   "Apparently," he said.

"Therefore," he said, "our souls are in Hades."

"It seems so."

"And doesn't one of the two becomings for these things happen to be a sure thing? For I take it dying is sure, isn't it?"

"Certainly," he said.

"What'll we do?" said he. "Shall we fail to give it the corresponding becoming that's contrary to it, and will nature instead be lame in this respect? Or is it necessary to give to dying some contrary becoming?"

"Entirely necessary, I suppose," he said.

"What is it?"

"Returning to life."

"Therefore," said he, "if in fact there is such a thing as returning to life, wouldn't this coming to be — this returning to life — be from the dead and into the living?"

72A

"Of course."

"So in this way too, we agree that the living have come to be from the dead no less than the dead from the living. And since this was the case, I suppose it seemed to be sufficient proof that it's necessary for the souls of the dead to *be* somewhere, whence they come to be again."

"Seems to me, Socrates," he said, "that it's necessarily so, given what we've agreed on."

"Then look at it this way, Cebes," he said, "and you'll see we did no injustice when we so agreed, as it seems to me. For if things that come to be didn't always make a return, each to its corresponding other, just as if they were going in a circle, but if instead becoming were a kind of straight line that proceeded only from one end to the directly opposite end and didn't bend back again towards its other or make any bend at all — do you know that all things would end up being in the same shape and would be affected in the same way and would stop coming to be?"

B

"What do you mean?" he said.

"It isn't at all hard," said he, "to take note of what I mean. For example, if there were falling asleep but no waking up again to correspond to and come to be from sleep, you know that all things would end up making nonsense of Endymion.[7] He'd make a poor showing, since all other things would be affected the same way he was — they'd all be asleep! And if all things were combined and not separated out, then the saying of Anaxagoras — 'All

C

[7] Endymion was an unusually beautiful boy, beloved by the moon and allowed to sleep forever.

things together' — would quickly have come about. And in the same way, my dear Cebes, if all things that partake of living were to die, and, when they died, the dead were to stay in that shape and not return to life, then wouldn't there be a great necessity for all things to end up dead and for nothing at all to be alive? For if the living were to come to be from anything other than the dead

D and the living were to die, what trick would there be to prevent all things from being utterly spent in death?"

"Seems to me not a single one, Socrates," said Cebes, "but in my opinion what you say is altogether true."

"Most definitely so, Cebes, as it seems to me," he said, "and we're not deceived in agreeing to these very things: There genuinely is a returning to life, the living come to be from the dead,

E and the souls of the dead *are*."

"And besides, Socrates," Cebes rejoined, "this also goes along with that other argument you're in the habit of making often, which — if it's true — says that our learning happens to be nothing other than recollection; and according to this argument, I sup-

73A pose it's necessary that we've learned at some previous time what we now recollect. But this is impossible if our soul was not somewhere before being born in this human form here. So in this way too the soul seems to be something deathless."

"But Cebes," Simmias rejoined, "what were the demonstrations for this? Remind me — I can't remember very well at present."

"There's one argument," said Cebes, "a most beautiful one: When human beings are questioned, if somebody questions them well, they themselves tell everything as it is, although if knowledge and a right account didn't happen to be within them, they wouldn't have been able to do this. Further, you get the surest indication that this is so when you direct them to mathematical

B diagrams or something else of that sort."[8]

"And if you're not persuaded by that, Simmias," said Socrates, "see if you don't come to the same opinion when you look at it in this way. You distrust — don't you — the claim that what's called learning is recollection?"

"It's not that I'm distrustful," said he, Simmias. "But I need," he said, "to undergo the very thing the account's about — recollecting. Though from what Cebes tried to say, I've already pretty

---

[8] In the *Meno* (82B ff.) Socrates questions a slave boy with the help of such a diagram and gets him to discover mathematical truths within himself.

nearly remembered and am persuaded. Still, I'd now like to hear how *you* were trying to put it."

C   "I was going to put it in this way," said he. "We agree, I suppose, that if anybody is to recollect anything, he must have knowledge of it at some time before."

"Of course," he said.

"Then do we also agree on this, that whenever knowledge comes to be present in this way, there's recollection? What way do I mean? This: Whenever somebody who's either seen or heard something — or has grasped it by some other sense — not only recognizes that thing but also takes note of another, the knowledge of which isn't the same but different, don't we justly say

D   that he recollects that of which he grasped the notion?"

"What do you mean?"

"Something like this: Knowledge of a human being and of a lyre are different, I suppose."

"Why, of course."

"Don't you know, then, that lovers, when they see a lyre or cloak or anything else that their boyfriend was in the habit of using, are affected in this way: They recognize the lyre and they grasp in thought the form of the boy whose lyre it was? And that's recollection. Just so, somebody who's seen Simmias often recollects Cebes. And there'd be a thousand such cases."

"A thousand, indeed, by Zeus!" said Simmias.

E   "Now isn't that sort of thing," said he, "a kind of recollection? Especially when somebody undergoes this concerning things which, from time and inattention, he'd already forgotten?"

"Certainly," he said.

"What about this?" said he. "Is it possible for somebody who's seen a sketched horse or a sketched lyre to recollect a human being, and who's seen Simmias sketched to recollect Cebes?"

"Of course."

"Then isn't it possible for somebody who's seen Simmias sketched to recollect Simmias himself?"

74A   "It's certainly possible," he said.

"Then doesn't it follow from all this that recollection stems from similar things and also stems from dissimilar?"

"It follows."

"But at least whenever somebody's recollecting something

from similar things, isn't it necessary for him to undergo this as well: to note whether or not, with respect to similarity, this thing somehow falls short of what he's recollected?"

"It's necessary," he said.

"Consider, then," said he, "if it's like this: We claim, I suppose, that there's some 'equal.' I don't mean stick equal to stick or stone to stone or anything else like that, but something other, beyond all these things — the Equal Itself. Shall we claim that this is something, or nothing at all?"

B   "By Zeus," said Simmias, "we certainly shall claim it, wondrously so!"

"And do we have knowledge of it, the Equal that *is*?"

"Of course," he said.

"And we grasped the knowledge of it from — where? Isn't it from the things we were talking about just now: We've seen sticks or stones or some other things that are equal, and from these we've noticed the Equal Itself, although it's other than these? Or doesn't it appear to you to be other? Look at the matter in this way: Isn't it the case that equal stones and sticks, while being the same, sometimes appear equal from one point of view and from another not?"

"Certainly."

C   "What about this: Is it possible that the Equals Themselves at times appeared to you to be unequals or Equality to be Inequality?"

"Never ever, Socrates."

"Therefore," said he, "these equals and the Equal Itself aren't the same."

"No way, as it appears to me, Socrates."

"And yet," he said, "it's nevertheless from these equals, although they're other than *that* Equal, that you've noted and grasped the knowledge of it?"

"What you say," he said, "is most true."

"And isn't it either similar or dissimilar to them?"

"Of course."

"But that makes no difference," said he. "So long as, after
D   you see one thing and from this sight you note something else, whether similar or dissimilar — that," he said, "must necessarily have been recollection."

"Certainly."

"What about this?" said he. "Do we undergo some such thing as this concerning equals among sticks and the other equals we were talking about just now: Do they appear to us to be equals in just the same way as the Equal Itself, the equal that *is*? Or do they fall somewhat short of being the sort of thing the Equal is — or not at all?"

"They fall short by a lot," he said.

E

"Then do we agree to this: Whenever somebody who's seen something notes, 'What I'm now seeing wants to be of the same sort as something else among the things that *are*; yet it falls short and isn't able to be that sort of thing but is inferior,' then mustn't the man who notes this necessarily have had occasion to see beforehand that thing he says it's like but falls short of?"

"Necessarily."

"Well then, have we too undergone some such thing with respect to equals and the Equal Itself, or not?"

"Altogether so."

75A

"Then it's necessary that we saw the Equal before that time when we first saw equals and noted: 'All these things are striving to be like the Equal but fall short of it.'"

"That's so."

"But surely we also agree on this: We haven't gotten the notion of it from somewhere else, nor is it even possible to get the notion of it except from seeing or touching or some other of the senses. And I say all these senses are the same thing."

"The same, Socrates, at least with respect to what the argument wants to make clear."

B

"So then, it's from the senses that we must get the notion that all the objects in these sensations both strive after the Equal that *is* and fall short of it. Is that what we're saying?"

"Just that."

"Therefore, before we began to see and hear and use the other senses, I suppose we must have had occasion to grasp the knowledge of the Equal Itself, the equal that *is*, if we were ever to refer There the equals that came from our senses and to think that all such things are putting their heart into being the sort of thing the Equal is but are inferior to it."

"That's necessary, from what we said before, Socrates."

"Weren't we both seeing and hearing and having the other

senses right from the moment we were born?"

"Of course."

C   "But, we declare, we must have grasped the knowledge of the Equal before all this?"

"Yes."

"Therefore, as it seems, it's necessary that we grasped it before we were born."

"So it seems."

"Then isn't this the case: If we grasped it and were born having it, we had knowledge both before we were born and right at the moment we were born, not only of the Equal and the Greater and the Less but also of all such things? For our present argument isn't about the Equal any more than it's about the Beautiful Itself and the Good Itself and the Just and the Holy and, as I say, about all those things upon which we set the seal 'that which *is*,' in the questions we ask as well as in the answers we give; so we must necessarily have grasped the various knowledges of all these things before we were born."

"That's so."

"And if in fact, after grasping these things, we didn't on each occasion forget them, then we're necessarily always born knowing them and know them throughout our life, since knowing is just this: when somebody who's grasped knowledge of something holds onto it and hasn't utterly lost it. Or don't we say that forgetting is just this, Simmias: the shedding of knowledge?"

E   "That's entirely so, Socrates," he said.

"But I suppose if, having grasped knowledge before we were born, we lost it utterly when we were born, but later by use of our senses we grasp again the various knowledges we once had before — then wouldn't what we call 'learning' be the grasping again of our old familiar knowledge? And I suppose we'd speak rightly if we called this 'recollecting?'"

"Of course."

76A   "For surely this appeared possible: A person senses something either by seeing or by hearing it or by grasping it with some other sense and — starting from this thing — notes some other he'd forgotten and which the sensed thing approaches, whether it's dissimilar or similar. So that, as I said, one or the other of two things holds. Either we were all born having knowledge of these things and have knowledge of them throughout our life; or we know later, and those of whom we say 'they learn' do nothing but recollect, and learning would be recollection."

"That's exactly how it is, Socrates."

"Then which do you choose, Simmias: Are we born already having knowledge, or do we recollect later things the knowledge of which we'd grasped before?"

"I can't choose at present, Socrates."

"Well now, surely you can choose between these, and have some sort of opinion about it: Can a man who has knowledge give an account of what he has knowledge of, or not?"

"There's a great necessity for this, Socrates," he said.

"And do all people seem to you to be able to give an account of those things we were talking about just now?"

"I sure wish they could," said Simmias. "But what I'm terrified of more than anything is that tomorrow at this time there'll no longer be anybody among human beings worthy of the task."

"Then, Simmias, I take it all people don't seem to you to have knowledge of these things?" he said.

"Not in the least."

"Then they recollect what they once learned?"

"That's a necessity."

"And our souls grasped the knowledge of these things — when? Surely not from the time we were born as human beings."

"Surely not."

"Therefore, it was before."

"Yes."

"Therefore, Simmias, our souls were earlier too, before they were in human form, and they were separate from bodies and had thoughtfulness."

"Unless, Socrates, we grasp these various knowledges as we are born — that time's still left."

"Well, my comrade — but at what other time do we lose them? For we aren't born having them, as we agreed just now. Or do we lose them at the very time we also grasp them? Or can you suggest some other time?"

*American Beauty — but then what would be the point?

"Not at all, Socrates — I was unaware that I wasn't making sense."

"Then is this our situation, Simmias?," he said. "If what we're

E forever babbling about *is* — some Beautiful as well as some Good and all such Being — and if we refer to this Being everything that comes from the senses, since we've discovered that it was present before and was ours, and if we liken the things of sense to that Being, then just as surely as these beings *are*, so also our soul *is*, even before we were born. And if they *are not*, then wouldn't this account we've given be beside the point? Is this our situation, and is there an equal necessity that these things *be* and that our souls *were* even before we were born, and if the former *are not*, then the latter *were not*?"

77A "Extraordinary, Socrates!" said Simmias, "There seems to me to be the same necessity, and the account is taking refuge in a beautiful conclusion: Our soul *is* before we were born, just as surely as the Being you spoke of just now. For my part, I've got nothing as lucid to me as this: All such things, Beautiful and Good and all the rest you were talking about just now, *are* as much as anything can be. And to me at any rate this point seems to have been sufficiently demonstrated."

"And to Cebes as well?" said Socrates. "For Cebes must be persuaded, too."

B "He's sufficiently persuaded — I think," said Simmias, "although he's the mightiest of men when it comes to distrusting arguments. But I imagine he hasn't failed to be persuaded that our soul *was* before we were born. And yet, Socrates," he said, "it doesn't seem, even to me myself, to have been demonstrated that when we die, the soul will still *be*. Instead, what Cebes was just talking about, the fear of the many, still threatens: When the human being dies, his soul is scattered, and this is the end of her being. For what keeps her from being born and being put together from somewhere or other and *being* before she arrives in a human body, and then, once she's arrived and is freed from the body, from reaching her end and being destroyed?"

C "Well put, Simmias," said Cebes. "For it appears that half, as it were, of what's needed has been demonstrated, namely, that our soul *was* before we were born. But it needs to be further demonstrated that when we die, our soul *will be* no less than she *was* before we were born — if the demonstration is to have an end."

"It's been demonstrated even now, Simmias and Cebes," said Socrates, "if you're willing to put this argument together with the one we agreed on before this: Every living thing comes to be
D from what's dead. For if the soul *is* beforehand as well, and if it's necessary for her, when she enters into life and is born, to come

to be from nowhere else than death and being dead, how is it not necessary for her to *be*, even when she's died, since she must be born again? Hence the very thing you were talking about just now has been demonstrated. All the same, it seems to me it would please you and Simmias to busy yourselves with the argument

E   some more, and besides, you have the fear of children — that in truth the wind will blow the soul away and scatter her in all directions as she departs from the body, especially whenever somebody happens to die, not in a calm, but in some great gust of wind."

And Cebes, with a laugh, said, "Try to persuade us as if we were afraid. Or rather, not as if *we* were afraid — perhaps even in us there's some child present who's terrified by such things. So let's try to persuade him not to fear death as if it were a hobgoblin."

"What you should do," said Socrates, "is to sing him incantations each day until you sing away his fears."

78A   "Then where, Socrates," he said, "are we to get hold of a good singer of such incantations, since you," he said, "are abandoning us?"

"There's a lot of Greece, Cebes," he said. "I suppose there are good men in it — and there are many races of foreigners too.[9] You must ransack them all in search of such a singer, sparing neither money nor toil, since there isn't anything more necessary on which you might spend your money. And you must search for him in company with one another, too, for perhaps you wouldn't easily find anyone more able to do this than yourselves."

B   "Then that's what we'll do," said Cebes. "But let's go back to where we abandoned the argument, if that gives you pleasure."

"It definitely gives me pleasure, how could it not?"

"Beautifully put," he said.

"Then mustn't we ask ourselves something like the following?" said Socrates. "What sort of thing is apt to suffer this affection — being scattered — and what sort of thing do we fear might suffer this? And what sort of thing is not apt to suffer it? And after this, must we not in turn investigate whether soul is of the one sort or the other, and from this whether we must be confident or fear for our soul?"

---

[9] The Greek word for foreigners is *barbaroi*. It refers to people whose speech has a mangled sound to Greek ears: "bar bar bar."

"What you say is true," he said.

C   "Now is what has been composed and is composite by nature apt to suffer this: to be divided up in just the way it was composed? And if anything turns out to be non-composite, isn't it alone, if anything, apt *not* to suffer this?"

"Seems to me to be that way," said Cebes.

"Then aren't those very things that are always self-same and keep to the same condition most likely to be non-composites; and aren't those that vary from one moment to another and are never in the self-same condition likely to be composites?"

"So it seems to me."

"Then let's go," he said, "to the very things we were talking about in the earlier argument. Does Being Itself — whose being we give an account of in our questioning and answering — always keep to the self-same condition, or does it vary from one moment to another? The Equal Itself, the Beautiful Itself, each thing itself that *is* — in short, that which *is* — do these ever admit of any sort of change whatsoever? Or does each thing that *is*, being of single form when taken itself all by itself, always keep to the self-same condition and never ever in any way whatsoever admit of any alteration at all?"

"It's necessarily in the self-same condition, Socrates," said Cebes.

E   "But what about the many beautiful things, such as human beings or horses or cloaks or any other such things of that sort, or equal things or anything else having the same names as those other things we mentioned? Do they keep to the self-same condition? Or, in complete contrast to those other things, are they, so to speak, never in any way self-same, either in relation to themselves or to each other?"

"That's how it is," said Cebes. "These in turn never keep to the same condition."

79A   "Now isn't it the case that you could touch and see and sense these by other senses, while it's not possible to grasp those things that always keep to the same condition other than by the reckoning of thought, since such things are unseen and not visible?"

"What you say is altogether true," he said.

"Let us then posit, if you want to," he said, "two forms of the things that *are* — the Visible and the Unseen."

"Let us posit them," he said.

"And posit that the Unseen always keeps to the self-same condition, while the Visible is never in the self-same condition?"

"Let us posit that as well," he said.

B   "Come then," said he, "is something of ourselves body and something else soul?"

"Nothing but," said he.

"Then to which form do we say the body would be more similar and akin?"

"This much is clear to everybody," he said, "that it's to the Visible."

"And what about the soul? Is she a visible or an unseen thing?"

"Unseen, at least by human beings, Socrates," he said.

"But surely we meant 'visible' and 'not visible' in relation to the nature of human beings , or do you think otherwise?"

"In relation to the nature of humans."

"Then what do we say about soul: Is she a visible or an invisible thing?"

"Not visible."

"Then she's unseen?"

"Yes."

"Therefore soul is a thing more similar to the Unseen than is body, and body more similar to the Visible."

C   "That's entirely necessary, Socrates."

"Now haven't we also been saying from way back that the soul, whenever she makes use of the body for investigating something, whether through seeing or through hearing or through any other sense (for that's what investigating through the body is — investigating something through sensing), then she's dragged by the body into things that never keep to the self-same condition, and she herself wanders and is shaken up and gets dizzy, just as if she were drunk, because she's had contact with such things?"

"Of course."

D   "But whenever, herself by herself, she investigates, she goes off There, to what's pure and *is* always and is deathless and keeps to the same condition, and since she's akin to this, continually comes to be with it — whenever, that is, she's come to be herself all by herself and this is possible for her — and then she's stopped her wandering and, around those things, always keeps to the self-same condition, because she's had contact with such things; and this state of hers has been called thoughtfulness — isn't all this so?"

"What you say is altogether beautiful and true, Socrates."

E

"So again, to which form does the soul seem to you to be more similar and akin, given what was said both before and now?"

"Everyone, it seems to me, even the slowest learner," said he, "must concede from this way of arguing that the soul is wholly and altogether more similar to what keeps to the same condition rather than to what doesn't."

"And what of the body?"

"It's similar to the other form."

80A

"Now see it in this way too: Whenever soul and body are in the same place, nature ordains the body to be a slave and to be ruled and the soul to rule and be master. Again, given this, which of the two seems to you to be similar to the divine and which to the deathbound? Or doesn't the divine seem to you to be of a nature to rule and govern and the deathbound to be ruled and be a slave?"

"Seems that way to me."

"Then which of the two is the soul like?"

"It's clear, Socrates, that the soul is like the divine and the body like the deathbound."

B

"Now consider, Cebes," he said, "whether these things follow for us from all that's been said: Soul is most similar to what's divine and deathless and intelligible and single-formed and indissoluble and always keeps to the self-same condition with itself. Body, in its turn, is most similar to what's human and deathbound and many-formed and unintelligible and dissoluble and never keeps to the self-same condition with itself. Can we say anything against this, my dear Cebes, to show that this conclusion doesn't hold?"

"We can't."

"Well then, since this is how things stand, isn't body apt to be dissolved quickly and soul in turn apt to be altogether indissoluble, or something close to this?"

C

"Why, of course."

"You note, then," he said, "that whenever the human being

dies, his visible part, lying in the visible realm, the body — which we call a corpse and which is apt to dissolve and fall apart and be dispersed — doesn't undergo any of these things right off but lasts for a rather long time, indeed for a very long time whenever somebody meets his end with his body in fine shape and at a fine time of year. For the body, when it's dried out and embalmed the way people are embalmed in Egypt, remains nearly whole for a remarkably long time. And when it rots, some parts of the body

D   — the bones and sinews and all such things — are still, so to speak, deathless. Isn't all this so?"

"Yes."

"And therefore the soul, that unseen thing that goes off to another region like herself, a region noble and pure and unseen — to the true Hades, the good and thoughtful god, where (god willing!) my soul too must soon go — will this soul of ours, being this sort of thing and having such a nature, be blown every which way and perish straightaway after she's freed from the body, as

E   the many say? Far from it, my dear Cebes, and Simmias too! Much rather is this the case: If she's set free pure, dragging along with her nothing of the body, because she was in no way willing to commune with it in life but fled it and gathered herself into herself, because she was always making this her care, which is nothing else but rightly philosophizing and exercising a ready care to

81A   be genuinely dead ... or wouldn't this be the care of death?"

"Altogether so."

"Then being in this condition, doesn't she go off to what's similar to her, to the Unseen — the divine and deathless and thoughtful — and once she arrives There, isn't it her lot to be happy, since she's been freed from wandering and mindlessness and terrors and savage loves and other human evils and, as is said of the initiates, truly spends the rest of time in the company of gods? Shall we say that, Cebes, or something else?"

"That, by Zeus!" said Cebes.

B   "But I imagine that if she's freed from the body defiled and impure, because she was always having intercourse with the body and servicing it and loving it and being bewitched by it and its desires and pleasures to the point that nothing else seemed true to her but what's body-like (which one can touch and see and drink and eat and use for the pleasures of love-making), and because she was in the habit of hating and trembling at and fleeing what's shadowy to the eyes and unseen but is intelligible and

C   seized on by philosophy — do you think a soul in this condition will be released herself all by herself and unadulterated?"

"In no way whatsoever," he said.

"But I take it she'll be set free pervaded by the body-like, which the company and intercourse with the body have made grow together with her because the soul was always with the body and gave it lots of care?"

"Of course."

"And, my friend, we should imagine that the body-like is oppressive and heavy and earthy and visible; and a soul in the sort of condition we described is made heavy and dragged back into the visible region through terror of the Unseen and of Hades

D   and, as they say, circulates among the memorials and tombs, around which certain shadowy apparitions of souls have been seen, ghostly images produced by the sort of souls that weren't released in purity but participate in the Visible — which is why they too are visible."

"That's likely, Socrates."

"Of course it's likely, Cebes. And it's not at all likely that these are the souls of the good — they're the souls of the inferior, souls compelled to wander around such places paying the penalty for

E   their former way of life, which was bad. And they wander about until, through the desire for the body-like that stalks them, they're again entangled in a body. And as is likely, they're entangled in whatever sort of characters they happen to have made their care in life."

"What sort of characters do you mean, Socrates?"

"I mean something like this: Those who've made gorgings and abusings and boozings their care and weren't wary of these things are likely to slip into the classes of donkeys and other such

82A   beasts. Don't you think so?"

"What you say is certainly likely."

"And those who held injustices and tyrannies and robberies in highest honor will slip into the classes of wolves and falcons and hawks — or where else do we say such souls would go?"

"Not to worry," said Cebes, "into such classes."

"Isn't it clear then," said he, "where all the rest would go as well, each one into a class that's similar to its care?"

"Why, certainly it's clear," he said.

B   "Then aren't the happiest of these, and the ones who go to
the best region," he said, "those who've devoted themselves to
the popular and political virtue people call moderation and justice, which is born of habit and of care, without philosophy and
without mind?"

"In what way are these the happiest?"

"Because it's likely that they'll arrive again into some such
political and tame class as perhaps that of bees or wasps or ants,
or even back again into the same human class, and from them
will be born temperate men."

"It's likely."

"And indeed it's not lawful for anybody who hasn't philoso-
C   phized and gone off from here entirely pure, to enter the class of
gods — but the lover of learning may. It is for these reasons, my
comrades Simmias and Cebes, that those who philosophize rightly
keep away from all the bodily desires and bear up and don't give
themselves over to them — not because they're somehow terrified of ruin and poverty, as are the many and money-loving; nor
again are they terrified of the dishonor and disrepute of corruption, as are the power-lovers and honor-lovers — not for that do
they keep away from desires."

"That, Socrates, wouldn't be fitting," said Cebes.

D   "No, it wouldn't be, by Zeus!" said he. "That, Cebes, is surely
why those who care for their own souls but don't live to serve the
body, bid farewell to all these people and don't make the same
journey as they do, since these others don't know where they're
going. But since they themselves consider that they must do nothing contrary to philosophy and to the release and cleansing it
effects, they turn to it and follow wherever it leads."

"How do they do that, Socrates?"

"I'll tell you," he said. "For the lovers of learning recognize,"
E   said he, "that when philosophy takes over their soul, she's utterly bound within the body and glued to it, and she's compelled
to investigate the things that *are* through it as through a cage rather
than herself through herself, and she wallows in every sort of
ignorance. And philosophy sees that the dreadful cleverness of
the cage comes from desire — so that the bound man would be
83A   himself the chief accomplice of his bondage. And so that's just
what I'm saying: Lovers of learning recognize that philosophy,
when it takes over their soul in this condition, gently persuades
her and attempts to release her. It shows her that investigation

through the eyes is full of deception, and that investigation through the ears and other senses is full of deception as well; and it persuades her to retreat from them, insofar as there's no necessity to use them. And philosophy exhorts her to gather and collect herself into herself and to trust in nothing but herself and

B   what she perceives herself all by herself of what's itself all by itself among the things that *are*, and to regard nothing else as true that she investigates through anything that's different from herself and differs under differing conditions. And it tells her that such a thing is sensible and visible, while what she herself sees is intelligible and invisible. Now the soul of the true philosopher thinks she must not run contrary to this release. And so she keeps herself away from pleasures and desires and pains and terrors as much as she can, reasoning that whenever somebody is violently pleased or terrified or pained or desirous, he doesn't just suffer

C   the evil one might think comes from them, such as falling ill or spending a lot because of desires. No, the greatest and most extreme evil of all — this he suffers, and it doesn't enter into his reasoning."

"What evil's that, Socrates?" Cebes said.

"That every human being's soul is compelled, at the very moment she's violently pleased or pained at something, to regard what above all brought about her suffering as both most manifest and most true — although this isn't the case. And these are above all visible things, aren't they?"

"Of course."

D   "Then in this experience above all, isn't soul tied down by body?"

"How's that?"

"Because each pleasure and pain — as if it had a nail — nails the soul to the body, pins her and makes her body-like, so she opines to be true exactly whatever things the body says are true. For as a result of her having similar opinions with the body and delighting in the same things, I imagine that the soul is compelled to become similar in ways and similar in nurture so as never to arrive in Hades pure; instead, she always leaves full of the body,

E   so that she tends to fall quickly again into another body and takes root there as if she had been sown. And as a result of this, she has no share of intercourse with the divine and pure and single-formed."

"What you say is most true, Socrates," said Cebes.

"Well then, it's for these reasons, Cebes, that those who are justly called lovers of learning are orderly and courageous — not for the reasons given by the many. Or do you suppose it's otherwise?"

84A   "I certainly don't."

"No indeed! A philosophic man's soul wouldn't reason it out that way: She wouldn't think that philosophy should release her and that, once released, she should of herself give herself over to pleasures and pains and tie herself down again to the body and engage in the unfinishable task of a Penelope unweaving the web she's woven.[10] No, instead his soul provides a calm sea untroubled by these things, follows reasoning and always abides in it, and beholds the true and the divine and the not-to-be-opined and is

B   nurtured by what she sees. That's how she thinks she must live while she's alive and how, when she meets her end, she'll arrive at what's akin to her and of her sort and be freed from human evils. And because her nurture has been of this sort, and since she has devoted herself to these things, there's no danger at all of her being terrified, Simmias and Cebes, that at the moment of her getting free of the body, she'll go off scattered and, all aflutter, be blown away by the winds and no longer be anywhere at all."

C   Silence came about when Socrates had said this, and it lasted a long time. And Socrates himself, to judge from looking at him, was absorbed in the previous argument, as were most of us. But Cebes and Simmias went on conversing with each other in a low voice, and Socrates saw the two of them and asked: "What is it?" he said. "You think there's something lacking in the previous argument, do you? Certainly, in many ways it's still open to suspicions and counterattacks — if, that is, somebody's going to go through it sufficiently. Now if you two are considering something else, I have nothing to say. But if you're perplexed about all this,

D   don't hesitate to speak up yourselves and go through it if it appears to you that it could've been said better. And what's more, don't hesitate to take me along with you if you think you'll fare better in my company."

And Simmias said: "Well, Socrates, I'll tell you the truth. For a long time now each of us has been perplexed and has been egg-

---

[10] In Homer's *Odyssey*, Penelope, while waiting out the ten years it takes for her husband Odysseus to return from the Trojan War, weaves a web during the day and undoes it at night. She thus hopes to escape marriage with the suitors infesting her house, one of whom she had promised to choose when the web was finished.

ing the other on and telling him to ask his question, because each of us had the desire to hear your answer but hesitated to make an uproar, for fear that it might be unpleasant for you in your present misfortune."

E

And when he heard this, he gave a gentle laugh and said: "Gosh, Simmias, I'd sure have a hard time persuading other human beings that I don't consider my present luck a misfortune, when I can't even persuade you two! No, you're terrified I might be somewhat crankier now than I was in my earlier life. And apparently I seem to you to be inferior in prophecy to the swans, who, although they sing at earlier times too, sing the most and

85A the most beautifully when they sense that they must die, in joy that they're about to go off to the very god whose servants they are. But humans, because of their fear of death, tell lies against the swans and say they sing out in pain, wailing for their death. And they don't reason that no bird sings when it's hungry or cold or is grieved by some other pain — not even the nightingale and the swallow and the hoopoe, who, they claim, are wailing in pain when they sing. But it doesn't appear to me that these birds

B sing because they're grieving — and neither do the swans. But since they belong to Apollo, they are, as I think, prophets and, because they have foreknowledge of the good things in Hades, they sing and make merry all that day far more than at any time before. Now I consider myself to be a co-servant with the swans and consecrated to the same god, and I think that I've received from our master a prophetic art no worse than theirs, and that I'm not being freed from life any more sad of heart than they. For that very reason, you should say and ask whatever you want — as long as the Athenian Eleven allow it."

C

"Beautifully put," said Simmias. "So I myself will tell you what perplexes me, and then this fellow here will in turn say in what way he doesn't accept what was said. It seems to me, Socrates, perhaps as it does to you too, that to know anything sure about such matters in our life now is either impossible or something altogether hard, while again, not to test in every way what's said about them and to back off before one is worn out with investigating them from every side, is the part of a really soft man. For in these matters, a man must, it seems to me, accomplish one of these things: He must learn or discover what's the case, or, if that's impossible, he must sail through life in the midst of danger, seizing on the best and the least refutable of human accounts, at any rate, and letting himself be carried upon

D   it as on a raft — unless, that is, he could journey more safely and less dangerously on a more stable carrier, some divine account. And so, for my part, I won't be ashamed to ask questions, since even you are telling me to do so, and I won't blame myself at a later time for not saying now what seems to me to be the case. For Socrates, when I consider what's been said, either within myself or with this fellow here, it's not altogether apparent to me that what was said was sufficient."

E   And Socrates said, "Perhaps, my comrade, what appears to you is true. But tell me exactly in what way it's not sufficient."

"In this way, as it seems to me," said he. "Somebody might also give the same account about a tuning and a lyre and its strings 86A — that the tuning is something invisible and bodiless and something altogether beautiful and divine in the tuned lyre, but that the lyre itself and its strings are bodies and are body-like and composite, and earth-like and are akin to the deathbound. Now what if, whenever somebody either shatters the lyre or cuts and breaks the strings, somebody should insist, by the very same argument you gave, that it's necessary that the tuning still *be* and not perish? For once the strings were broken, there'd be no trick by which the lyre and strings could still be, since they're deathbound in form; and no trick by which the tuning could per- B   ish — and perish before that deathbound thing — since it's naturally similar and akin to the divine and deathless. Instead, he'd claim it's necessary that the tuning itself still *be* somewhere and that the wood and strings rot before the tuning suffers in any way. For I certainly suppose, Socrates, that you've gathered that we take the soul to be just this sort of thing — that while our body is strung and held together by warm and cold and dry and wet and the like, our soul is, as it were, a blend and tuning of C   these very things, whenever, that is, they're blended with one another in a beautiful and measured way. If, then, the soul turns out to be some sort of tuning, it's clear that whenever our body is relaxed or strained without measure by diseases and other evils, it's a necessity that the soul perish right away, even though she's most divine — just as do other 'tunings' in sounds and in all the works of craftsmen — while the remains of each body stick around D   for a long time, until they're burned or rot. See, then, what we'll say in response to this argument, if somebody maintains that the soul — since she's a blend of the elements of the body — is, in what's called death, the first to perish."

Then, with that usual keen look of his and a smile, Socrates said, "What Simmias is saying is certainly just. So if one of you is better provided than I am, why not answer? Now surely Simmias is like somebody who's got no mean hold on the argument! And yet it seems to me that before his answer we should first listen to Cebes, to hear *his* charge against the argument. That way, as time goes by, we may take counsel on what we're to say, and then, once we've listened, either concede to them, if they strike the proper note, or, if they don't, continue our advocacy of the argument. But come, Cebes," said he, "you tell us what was shaking you up."

E

"I'll tell you," said Cebes. "For to me the argument still appears to be at the same point, and the very same charge we were talking about earlier holds. I don't take back that it's been demonstrated with complete elegance and, if it's not laying it on too thick, complete adequacy, that our soul *was* even before she came into her present form. But that she'll still *be* somewhere after we've died — this does not seem to me to have been so demonstrated. I don't grant Simmias' objection, that soul isn't a stronger and more long-lasting thing than body, for it seems to me she's vastly superior in all these respects. 'Why, then,' the argument might say, 'are you still distrustful, since you see that after the human being's died his weaker part still *is*? Doesn't it seem to you necessary that the more long-lasting part still be kept safe and sound during this time?' Now consider whether my reply to just this point amounts to anything. And it seems I too need some sort of likeness, just as Simmias did. For what's been said about the soul seems to me similar to what somebody might argue about an old weaver-man who'd died: that the human hadn't perished but continued to *be* somewhere, safe and sound. And he'd offer as proof of this that a cloak the fellow used to wear and which he himself had woven was safe and sound and hadn't perished; and if somebody distrusted him, he'd ask which class was more long-lasting, that of a human or of a cloak in constant use and wear; and when the person answered 'Of a human, by far,' he'd think he had demonstrated that therefore the human being is most certainly safe and sound, since the less long-lasting hadn't perished. But what I think, Simmias, is that the argument doesn't hold up — for you too consider what I'm saying. Anybody could grasp that the man who talks that way talks simple-mindedly. For this weaver who wore out and wove many such cloaks perished later than they did, even though the cloaks were many, but he did so, I suppose, earlier than the last one; and for all that, a human

87A

B

C

D

being's in no way inferior to a cloak, nor is he weaker. Now I think soul in relation to body would admit of the same likeness, and somebody who said the same thing about them would appear to me to speak sensibly when he said that the soul's more

E   long-lasting while the body's weaker and less long-lasting. But should he go on to say that each of our souls wears out many bodies, especially if a life lasted many years — that is, if the body's going to be in flux and perishing while the human being's still living, but the soul's always going to re-weave what wears out — then surely it'd be necessary for the soul, at whatever time she might perish, to happen to have on her last weave and to perish earlier than this one alone; and when the soul had perished, the body would from that moment on show the nature of its weak-

88A   ness and, rotting quickly, would go off. So that anybody who trusts this argument isn't yet worthy of the confidence he has that when we die our soul will still *be* somewhere. For if one were to concede even more than what you say to somebody who makes this argument, granting him not only that our souls *were* in the time before we were born but also that nothing prevents this — that the souls of some of us, once we're dead, still *are* and *will be* and will often be born and die in turn (because a soul is so strong a thing by nature that she can withstand being born often) — even if one granted this, one might not go on to concede that she doesn't exhaust herself in these many births and, meeting her end in one of these deaths, doesn't perish altogether. But one would claim that nobody knows the particular death and dissolution of the

B   body that brings destruction to the soul. For this is impossible for any of us to perceive. But if all this holds, the confidence that characterizes anybody who's confident in the face of death is a mindless confidence — so long as he can't demonstrate that the soul is altogether deathless and imperishable. And if he cannot, then it's necessary that a man about to die always fear for his soul, in case she should altogether perish in her imminent unyoking from the body."

C   Now once we'd heard what they said, all of us felt ill at ease (as we told one another later) because, after we'd been so power-fully persuaded by the previous argument, they now seemed to shake us up again and to cast us back into distrust, concerning not only the arguments that came before but even what would be said later on. Who knows, we might be worthless judges, or these matters themselves might even be beyond trust!

Echecrates: By the gods, Phaedo, I have real sympathy for all of

you! For as I myself now listen to you, it occurs to me to say something like this to myself: "What argument will we trust from now
D   on? The one that was so powerfully trustworthy — the argument
that Socrates gave — has now fallen into discredit." For this argument, that our soul is a sort of tuning has now, as ever, a wonderful hold on me, and your speaking of it reminded me, as it
were, that up till now all this seemed to be the case to me too.
And now what I really need is some other argument which will,
from a new beginning as it were, persuade me that when somebody dies, the soul won't die along with him. So tell me, by Zeus,
in what direction did Socrates pursue the argument? And which
E   was it: Did he too, as you say the rest of you did, reveal in any
way that he was distressed; or didn't he, and did he instead come
serenely to the aid of the argument? And was his aid sufficient,
or did it fall short? Go through everything for us as precisely as
you can.

Phaedo: Although, Echecrates, I'd often wondered at Socrates, I
never admired him more than when I was present with him then.
89A   That he should have something to say was perhaps not out of the
ordinary. No, what I really wondered at him for was this: first,
how pleasantly and kindly and admiringly he received the young
men's argument, then how keenly he perceived how we'd suf-
fered under their arguments, then how well he healed us and, as
if we were men who'd fled and been laid low, rallied us and turned
us about to follow him and consider the argument with him.

Echecrates: How did he do it?

B   **Phaedo:** I'll tell you. I happened to be sitting to his right on a sort
of low stool next to the couch, and he was on a seat a lot more
elevated than mine. And he caressed my head and gathered up
the hair on my neck — for he was in the habit, on occasion, of
teasing me about my hair — and said, "Tomorrow, Phaedo, perhaps you'll cut off these beautiful locks of yours."[11]

"That's likely, Socrates," said I.

"Not if you're persuaded by me."

"Then what?" said I.

"This very day," he said, "I'll cut mine, and you'll cut these
locks of yours, if our argument meets its end and we can't bring
it back to life. And as for me, if I were you and the argument were
C   to get away from me, I'd make an oath, as did the Argives, not to

---

[11] The Greeks cut off their hair when in mourning.

cut my hair before I should be victorious in the renewed battle against the argument of Simmias and Cebes."

"But," said I, "they say not even Heracles could manage against two."[12]

"Then call on me as well," he said, "as your Iolaus — while there's still light."

"Well then, I will call on you," I said, "not as a Heracles but as an Iolaus calling on Heracles."

"Makes no difference," he said. "But first let's be on our guard so we don't undergo a certain experience."

"What sort of experience?" said I.

D   "So that we don't become," said he, "haters of argument, as some become haters of human beings; for it's not possible," he said, "for anybody to experience a greater evil than hating arguments. Hatred of arguments and hatred of human beings come about in the same way. For hatred of human beings arises from artlessly trusting somebody to excess, and believing that human being to be in every way true and sound and trustworthy, and then a little later discovering that this person is wicked and untrustworthy — and then having this experience again with another. And whenever somebody experiences this many times, and especially at the hands of just those he might regard as his most E   intimate friends and comrades, he then ends up taking offense all the time and hates all human beings and believes there's nothing at all sound in anybody. Or haven't you perceived that something like this happens?"

"Of course," said I.

"Isn't it shameful," said he, "and clear that such a person was attempting to deal with human beings without art in human affairs? For if he dealt with them artfully, he'd think of them just 90A   as they are — that both the really good-natured and the really wicked are few, and that most people are in between."

"What are you saying?" said I.

"Just what I'd say if we were talking about the really small

---

[12] Heracles was the most admired of Greek heroes, who performed twelve prodigious labors, most of them concerned with slaying monsters and conquering death. Iolaus was his young companion in these exploits. In the dialogue *Euthydemus* (297C) Socrates recalls in the midst of an argument that Heracles had to summon Iolaus to help him fight the many-headed Hydra and a second sea-monster.

and the really big," he said. "Do you suppose anything's more rare than finding either a really big or a really small man or dog or any other such thing, or again, one that's really fast or slow, or really ugly or beautiful, or really white or black? Haven't you perceived that among all such things those at the farthest ends of either extreme are rare and few, while the ones in between are in generous supply and many?"

"Of course," said I.

B   "And don't you think," he said, "that if a wickedness contest were held, those who showed first would be very few here as well?"

"That's likely," said I.

"Likely indeed," he said. "Now arguments aren't similar to human beings in that respect — I was merely following your lead just now — but rather in this one: when somebody trusts some argument to be true without the art of arguments, and then a little later the argument seems to him to be false, as it sometimes is and sometimes isn't, and this happens again and again with one argument after another. And, as you know, those especially

C   who've spent their days in debate-arguments end up thinking they've become the wisest of men and that they alone have detected that there's nothing sound or stable — not in the realm of either practical matters *or* arguments — but all the things that *are* simply toss to and fro, as happens in the Euripus, and don't stay put anywhere for any length of time."[13]

"Certainly," said I, "what you say is true."

"Then, Phaedo," he said, "his condition would be a pitiable one if, when there was in fact some argument that was true and

D   stable and capable of being detected, somebody — through his associating with the very sort of arguments that sometimes seem to be true and sometimes not — should not blame himself or his own artlessness but should end up in his distress being only too pleased to push the blame off himself and onto the arguments, and from that moment on should finish out the rest of his life hating and reviling arguments and should be robbed of the truth and knowledge of the things that *are*."

"Yes, by Zeus," I said, "pitiable indeed!"

E   "Then first of all," he said, "let's be on our guard against this

---

[13] The Euripus, a narrow sea-channel between the Greek mainland and the island of Euboea, reverses its direction at least seven times a day.

condition and not admit into the soul that the realm of arguments risks having nothing sound in it. Instead let's far rather admit that *we're* not yet sound but must act like men and put our hearts into being sound — you and the others for the sake of your whole life hereafter, and I for the sake of death itself. For at present, as far as that goes, I run the risk of being in a mood not to love wisdom but to love victory, as do altogether uneducated people. These people, whenever they dispute about something, don't give a thought to the way it is with the things the argument's about, but put their hearts into this: that what they themselves put forward should seem to be the case to those present. And at present I seem to myself to differ from those people in this way only: I won't put my heart into making what I say seem to be true to those present, except as a side effect, but into making it seem to be the case to me myself as much as possible. For I'm calculating, my dear comrade — behold how self-servingly! — that if what I'm saying happens to be true, I'm well off believing it; and if there's nothing at all for one who's met his end, well then, I'll make myself so much the less unpleasant with lamenting to those who are present during this time, the time before my death; and this mindlessness of mine won't continue — that would be an evil! — but will perish a little later. Thus prepared, Simmias and Cebes," he said, "I enter on the argument. But as for all of you, if you're persuaded by me and give little thought to Socrates and much more to the truth, you must agree with me if I seem to you to say what's true; and if I don't, you must strain against me with every argument you've got, taking care that I don't, out of eagerness, go off, having deceived both myself and you, like a bee that's left its stinger behind.

"But we must get going," he said. "First remind me of what you were saying, in case it's apparent that I haven't remembered it. Simmias, as I think, is distrustful and is terrified that the soul, though she's a more divine and beautiful thing than the body, may perish before it, if she's in the form of a tuning. And Cebes seemed to me to concede to me that soul was much more long-lasting than body, but claimed that the following's unclear to everybody: whether, having often worn out many bodies, the soul, once she's left the last body, does not now perish herself, and this very thing is death — perishing of soul — since body of course never stops perishing. Anything other than these points, Simmias and Cebes, that we must investigate?"

The pair agreed that these were the points.

"Now is it that you don't accept," he said, "all the previous arguments, or do you accept some and not others?"

"Some we do, some we don't," said the two.

92A "What do you say, then," said he, "about the former argument where we claimed that learning is recollection and that — if this holds — it necessarily holds that our soul *is* somewhere else earlier, before she's bound within the body?"

"I was wonderfully persuaded by it then," Cebes said, "and I stick with it now as with no other argument."

"I myself am certainly in that situation, too," Simmias said, "and I'd be filled with wonder if I ever had a different opinion about this matter."

And Socrates said, "But it's necessary that you have different opinions, my Theban guest, as long as this thought of yours sticks around — that a tuning is a composite thing and soul a sort of tuning composed of bodily elements tensed like strings. For you won't, I suppose, allow yourself to say that a tuning was composed before those things *were*, from which it had to be composed. Or will you allow it?"

"No way, Socrates," he said.

"Do you perceive, then," said he, "that you're going to be saying this whenever you claim that the soul *is* before she arrives in human form and body and that she's composed of things that *are not* yet. For in fact a tuning's not the sort of thing you liken it to. Instead, the lyre and the strings and the sounds come into being earlier, while they're still untuned, and the tuning is the last of all to be composed and the first to perish. Then how will this argument of yours sing in accord with that other one?"

"It won't at all," said Simmias.

"And yet," said he, "it's fitting that it be in accord with the argument about tuning if with any!"

"It's fitting," Simmias said.

"Well then," he said, "this one of yours doesn't sing in accord. But see which of the two arguments you prefer — that learning is recollection or soul a tuning."

"The first, Socrates, by a long shot," he said. "The other came to me without demonstration and with a certain likelihood and attractiveness — which is also why it seems to be the case to many human beings. And I know that arguments that make their demonstrations through likelihoods are impostors, and if one doesn't have one's guard up against them, they do quite a good job of deceiving us, both in geometry and in everything else. But the recollection and learning argument was established through a hypothesis worthy of being accepted. For it was established, I suppose, that our soul *is* even before arriving in the body, just as certainly as that Being she belongs with has the title 'that which *is*.' And this Being, I persuade myself, I've accepted for adequate

E   and right reasons. Then because of all this, it's necessary for me, as it seems, to allow neither myself nor anyone else to say that soul is a tuning."

"What about this way of looking at it, Simmias?" said he.

93A   "Does it seem to you that a tuning or any other composition is apt to be in some other condition than whatever the condition is of the things from which it's composed?"

"No way."

"Nor, as I think, is it apt to do or suffer anything else beyond what those things may do or suffer?" He gave his assent.

"Therefore a tuning is apt not to lead these things from which it's composed, but to follow them." He went along with this opinion.

"Therefore it's far from being the case that a tuning undergoes contrary movement or makes contrary sounds, or does anything else that runs contrary to its parts."

"Far from it indeed."

"Well then, isn't each tuning by nature a tuning insofar as it's been tuned?"

"I don't understand," he said.

"Wouldn't it be more so and more fully a tuning," said he, "if

B   — allowing that this could happen — it could be tuned more so and more fully, and less so and less fully a tuning if it were tuned less so and less fully?"

"Of course."

"Then is this the same case with soul? Is one soul, even in the slightest degree, more fully and more so than another, or less fully and less so this very thing — a soul?"

"In no way whatever," he said.

"Well then, by Zeus!" he said. "Is one soul said to have both mind and virtue and to be good, while another has both mind-

C   lessness and wickedness and is bad? And is what's said true?"

"True indeed."

"So what will one of those who posit soul as tuning claim these things in our souls are — virtue and vice? That they in turn are some other tuning and lack of tuning? And that the one soul, the good one, has been tuned and has another tuning in herself, although she's already a tuning, while the other soul is untuned and has no other tuning within herself?"

"I myself can't say," said Simmias, "but it's clear that the one who held that hypothesis would be saying some such thing."

D   "But it was agreed earlier," he said, "that one soul is neither more nor less a soul than another; and that amounts to the agreement that one tuning is neither more so and more fully nor less so and less fully a tuning than another. Isn't that so?"

"Of course."

"And that which is neither more nor less a tuning is neither more nor less tuned. Is that so?"

"It is."

"But as for that which is neither more nor less tuned, does it partake of tuning any more or less fully, or does it do so equally?"

"Equally."

"Then as for soul, since one is neither more nor less than an-
E   other this very thing — soul — isn't she neither more nor less tuned?"

"That's so."

"And, since this is her condition, she couldn't partake more fully of either lack of tuning or tuning?"

"No, she couldn't."

"And moreover, since this is her condition, one soul couldn't partake of vice or of virtue any more fully than another, if in fact vice is to be lack of tuning and virtue tuning?"

"No more fully."

"And I suspect it's rather the case, Simmias, that not a single
94A   soul, according to the right account, will partake of vice, if in fact she's a tuning. For since a tuning, I presume, is entirely this very thing — a tuning — it couldn't ever partake of lack of tuning."

"Certainly not."

"Nor, I presume, could soul, in being altogether soul, partake of vice."

"How could it, from what was said before?"

"Therefore it follows from this argument of ours that all souls of all living beings will similarly be good if in fact it's similarly the nature of souls to be this very thing — souls."

"That seems so to me, Socrates."

"Now does this seem to you to be a fine way to talk," said he, "and does it seem that the argument would suffer this, if the hypothesis were right that soul is a tuning?"

"In no way fine," he said.

"Now what about this," said he, "of all the things in a human being, do you claim that anything else rules but soul, especially if she's thoughtful?"

"Not I."

"And which of these do you claim: that she gives way to the passions of the body or that she runs contrary to them? Here's what I mean: When the body has burning heat and thirst within it, doesn't she drag it in the contrary direction, toward not drinking, and when the body has hunger within it, toward not eating? And I suppose we see the soul running contrary to what belongs to the body in a thousand other ways, don't we?"

"Certainly."

"But didn't we agree previously that if she were a tuning, she could never sing out in a way that runs contrary to those things out of which she happens to be constituted — whether they were tensed or relaxed or plucked, or whatever other condition they might undergo — but she'd follow them and never govern them?"

"Why, course we agreed," he said.

"Well then, doesn't the soul now appear to us as working in an altogether contrary way, governing all those things out of which somebody might claim she was constituted, and running contrary to just about all of them throughout all our life and being their master in all ways — disciplining some more harshly and with pain, as do gymnastics and medicine, and others more gently, threatening some while admonishing others and talking with desires and tempers and terrors as if she were other than they and had a task other than theirs? As Homer too has put it poetically in the *Odyssey*, where he says of Odysseus:

> He struck his breast and reproached his heart with this word:
> 'Bear up my heart, for at other times you've borne things even
> more fit for a dog.'[14]

---

[14] *Odyssey* XX 17-18. This passage is cited by Socrates in the *Republic* (390D and 441B) as an example of self-mastery.

Do you suppose he made this poetry with the thought in mind that soul is a tuning and is of the sort to be led by the passions of the body; or rather that she's of the sort to lead them and be their master, and is herself a far more divine thing than she would be as a tuning?"

"By Zeus, Socrates, that's how it seems to me!"

95A   "Therefore, my excellent friend, we're in no way putting it in a fine way when we say that soul is some sort of tuning. For then it's likely that we'd be agreeing neither with Homer, the Divine Poet, nor with ourselves."

"That's how things stand," he said.

"Well then," said Socrates, "somehow that business with Harmonia the Theban goddess has, as it seems, grown fairly gracious to us. But what about that business with Cadmus, Cebes?" he said. "How are we going to make it gracious — and by what argument?"[15]

B   "Seems to me you'll discover a way," Cebes said. "At any rate, in my view you managed this argument against tuning wondrously and beyond all expectation. For as Simmias was explaining what perplexed him, I was really wondering if anyone would be able to deal with his argument. That's why it seemed really absurd to me that right off it failed to resist the first assault of your argument. So I wouldn't wonder if the argument of Cadmus too should suffer the same fate."

C   "Ah, my good man," Socrates said, "don't boast — we don't want some witchery to rout the argument we're about to make. But these matters will be in the god's care; as for us, let's come to close quarters in Homeric style and try to see if there's anything to what you're saying. The upshot of what you're searching for is this: You demand that our soul be shown to be both imperishable and deathless — if, that is, a philosophic man who's about to die, and who's confident and believes he'll do well There once he's dead, better than if he'd ended his lives in a different life, is not to be confident with a confidence both mindless and stupid. And as for our making apparent that the soul is something strong and godlike and that she *was* even before we became humans — nothing, you say, prevents this from evidencing not deathlessness, but

[15] Harmonia, the daughter of Ares, the god of war, and Aphrodite, the goddess of love, was the first queen of Thebes, Simmias' and Cebes' home city. Her name is that of the musical term translated here as "tuning." Cadmus was her husband, the legendary founder of Thebes. He was said to have brought writing to Greece. Note that Socrates is about to talk of his book-learning.

only that soul is long-lasting and *was* somewhere earlier for an unbelievably long time and both knew and did a great many things. But surely not for all that is she something deathless; instead, her very entering into a human body was, like a disease, the beginning of her perishing. She lives this life wearing herself out in misery and ends up perishing in what's called death. Now you say it makes no difference at all, as far as each of us being terrified goes, whether she enters once into a body or many times; being terrified befits anyone who doesn't know that she's something deathless and who can't give an account — unless he's mindless. I suppose you're saying something like that, Cebes. And I purposely keep going back over things often so that nothing may escape us and so that, if you want, you may add or take away something."

And Cebes said, "But at present there's nothing I need to take away or add; that's just what I'm saying."

Then Socrates paused for a long time and within himself considered something and said, "What you're searching for is no trivial business, Cebes. For we must busy ourselves with the cause concerning generation and destruction as a whole. So I'll go through my own experiences about them for you, if you want me to. Then, should something of what I have to say appear useful to you, you can use it for purposes of persuasion in the very matters you're talking about."

"But I do want you to," said Cebes.

"Listen then and I shall tell you. For I, Cebes," he said, "as a young man was wondrously desirous of that wisdom they call 'inquiry into nature.'[16] This wisdom seemed to me grandiose — to know the causes of each thing, why each thing comes to be and why it perishes and why it *is*; and very often I cast my thought to and fro looking first of all into questions like these: Is it when hot and cold bring about a certain fermentation, as some people say, that animals grow into organisms? And is the blood that by which we're thoughtful? Or is it air or fire? Or is it none of these, and is it the brain that produces the senses of hearing and seeing and smelling; and would memory and opinion arise out of these, and in this way out of memory and opinion brought to a state of rest arises knowledge? And then in turn, I looked into the processes by which these things pass away and the affections that pertain to heaven and earth, until I ended up with the opinion

---

[16] In Aristophanes' *Clouds*, Socrates is lampooned for his acquaintance with the opinions of the so-called "physicists," who speculated on the constitution of the visible world (225 ff.).

that my natural fitness for this 'looking into things' was next to nothing. And I'll give you sufficient proof of this. It concerns what

C I had sure knowledge of even before, in my opinion at least and in the opinion of others — I was so intensely blinded by this 'looking' that I unlearned even what I thought I knew before about many other things and about why a human being grows. Before I used to think this was clear to everybody: that a human being grows because of eating and drinking. For when, from the food he eats, amounts of flesh are attached to flesh and amounts of

D bone to bones, and so in this way by the same account what's congenial to his other parts gets attached to them, then the bulk that's little has later become a lot and in this way the small human being becomes big. That's what I used to think then. Don't I seem sensible to you?"

"To me you do, yes," said Cebes.

"Then look at this further thing too. I used to think the following opinion of mine was sufficient: that whenever a big fellow appeared standing next to a small one, he was larger by just this, a head, and that one horse was bigger than another for the same

E reason. And to mention things even more lucid, it seemed to me that ten things were more than eight because two were added to the eight; and it seemed to me that a two-foot length was larger than a one-foot length because it exceeded it by half of itself."

"And now," said Cebes, "how do these things seem to you?"

"By Zeus!" he said, "I seem to be far from thinking, I suppose, that I know the cause concerning any of these things, I who don't even allow myself to assert that whenever anyone adds a one to a one, the one added to or the one that was added has become two, or that the one that was added and the one to which it was added became two by the addition of the one to the other.

97A Here's what I wonder about: When each of the two was separate from the other, then each was one and the pair were not two, but when they came close to each other, this then became the cause of their becoming two — the concourse that comes from their being placed close to each other. Nor again can I yet be persuaded that if somebody splits a one apart, this — the splitting — has in turn

B become the cause of their having become two. For then this cause comes to be the contrary of the former cause of their becoming two. Then it was because they were led close to one another and were added, one to the other, but now it's because they're led away and separated one from the other. Nor do I any longer even persuade myself that I know why a one comes to be nor why, in a word, anything else comes to be or perishes or *is* by this way of proceeding. Instead, I've randomly smushed together another way myself, and that former one I don't tolerate at all.

C

D

E

98A

B

Once, though, I heard somebody reading from a book he said was by Anaxagoras and which said that it is in fact Mind that puts the world in order and is responsible for all things.[17] Now I was pleased with this sort of cause, and it seemed to me in some way good that Mind should be responsible for all things. And I considered that if this is the case, then Mind at least, in ordering the world, would order all things and position each thing in just that way which was best. So if somebody should want to discover the cause concerning each thing — in what way it comes into being or perishes or *is* —he'd have to discover this concerning it: in what way it's best for it either to be or to undergo or do anything whatsoever. Now by this account, it befits a human being, in this matter and in all others, to look to nothing but what's most excellent and best. And then this same human being necessarily knows what's worse as well; for the knowledge concerning these is the same. As I reasoned these things out, I thought I had discovered, to my great pleasure, a teacher after my own mind, a teacher of the cause concerning the things that *are* — Anaxagoras. I thought he'd tell me first whether the earth was flat or round, and when he had told me that, he'd go on to take me through the cause and necessity of it, saying what's better and why in particular it's better for the earth to be such as it is. And if he claimed that it was in the middle, he'd go on to take me through how it was better for it to be in the middle. And if he could make these things apparent to me, I was prepared to yearn no longer for any other form of cause. What's more, I was prepared to find out about the sun in just the same way and about the moon and the rest of the heavenly bodies, both about their speeds relative to one another and their turning points and their other affections, too — in what way it's better for each to do and undergo what it undergoes. For I'd never have supposed — when he alleged they'd been ordered by Mind — that he'd impute to them any other cause than that it's best for them to be in just the condition they're in. Thus, once he'd given the cause for each one and for all of them in common, I thought he'd go on to take me through the best for each and the good common to all. I wouldn't

---

[17] Anaxagoras, who belonged to the generation before Socrates, was the first non-Athenian thinker concerned with the nature of things to settle and teach in Athens. Like Socrates, he was prosecuted by Athens for impiety.

have given up my hopes for anything. Instead, after getting hold of the books with all haste, I read them as speedily as I could so that I might know as speedily as possible the best and the worse.

"From this wonderful hope, my comrade, I was swept away, since, as I went on with my reading, I saw a man who didn't employ Mind at all and didn't hold any causes responsible for putting things in order, but instead put the blame on air and ether and water and other things many and absurd.[18] And to me his condition seemed most similar to that of somebody who — after saying that Socrates does everything he does by mind and then venturing to assign the causes of each of the things I do — should first say that I'm now sitting here because my body's composed of bones and sinews, and because bones are solid and have joints keeping them separate from one another, while sinews are such as to tense and relax and also wrap the bones all around along with the flesh and skin that holds them together. Then since the bones swing in their sockets, the sinews, by relaxing and tensing, make me able, I suppose, to bend my limbs right now — and it's through this cause that I'm sitting here with my legs bent. And again, as regards my conversing with you, he might assign other causes of this sort, holding voices and air and sounds and a thousand other such things responsible, and not taking care to assign the true causes — that since Athenians judged it better to condemn me, so I for my part have judged it better to sit here and more just to stay put and endure whatever penalty they order. Since — by the Dog![19] —these sinews and bones of mine would, I think, long ago have been in Megara or Boeotia, swept off by an opinion about what's best, if I didn't think it more just and more beautiful, rather than fleeing and playing the runaway, to endure whatever penalty the city should order.[20] But to call such things causes is too absurd. If somebody should say that I wouldn't be able to do what seemed best to me without having such things as bones and sinews and whatever

C

D

E

99A

---

[18] Socrates echoes Odysseus, who was swept back out to sea within sight of home by the folly of his companions (*Odyssey* X 48).

[19] The oath "by the Dog!" is Socrates' very own, which he uses quite often. In the *Gorgias* he makes it clear that it is the dog-headed god, Anubis of Egypt, he is invoking (482B). Anubis, like his Greek counterpart Hermes, had the role of mediating between earth and underworld, the living and the dead.

[20] In the dialogue named after him, Socrates' friend Crito tries to persuade Socrates, who is awaiting his execution in prison, to escape. He tells him that Simmias and Cebes have brought funds to get him out, to Boeotian Thebes or some other city. In the rest of the dialogue Socrates shows Crito why he must refuse to run away.

else I've got, he'd be speaking the truth. If, however, he should say it was *through* these things that I'm doing what I'm doing, engaging in these acts by mind but not by the choice of what's best, why the slackness of his speech would be abundant and tedious. Imagine not being able to distinguish that it's one thing to be genuinely the cause, and another to be that without which the cause wouldn't be a cause! In this respect it's apparent to me that the many are groping around as if in the dark when they apply to the latter an improper name and address it as cause. And this is also why one man makes the earth stay put under the heaven by placing a vortex around the earth, and why another props it up on a pedestal of air, as though it were on a wide kneading-trough. But as for the power of placing things as they are now situated — in the best way possible — this power they don't search for, nor do they think it's got any superhuman strength; but they believe that some day they'll discover an Atlas stronger and more deathless than this one, one who'd do a better job of holding all things together. And they don't at all suppose it's the Good-and-Binding that truly binds and holds things together. Now for that sort of cause — how it works — it'd be a pleasure to become anybody's student. But since I was robbed of this and never became capable of discovering it myself or learning it from another, do you want me to make a display, Cebes," he said, "of the way by which I've busied myself with the second sailing in search of the cause?"[21]

"Yes, I want you to," he said, "extraordinarily so!"

"Well then after these experiences," said he, "since I had had it with this looking into beings, it seemed to me I had to be on my guard so as not to suffer the very thing those people do who behold and look at the sun during an eclipse. For surely some of them have their eyes destroyed if they don't look at the sun's likeness in water or in some other such thing. I thought this sort of thing over and feared I might be totally soul-blinded if I looked at things with my eyes and attempted to grasp them by each of the senses. So it seemed to me that I should take refuge in accounts and look in them for the truth of beings.[22] Now perhaps in a certain way it isn't quite like what I'm likening it to. For I don't at all concede that somebody who looks into beings in accounts looks at them in likenesses to a greater extent than one who does so in actions. In any case, that's how I set out: On each occasion I

B

C

D

E

100A

---

[21] The "second sailing" refers to the use of oars when the wind fails.

[22] "Accounts" renders the plural of *logos*. For the range of meaning of this important term, see Glossary, p. 102.

put down as hypothesis whatever account I judge to be mightiest; and whatever seems to me to be consonant with this, I put down as being true, both about cause and about all the rest, while what isn't, I put down as not true. But I want to tell you more plainly what I mean, because I think that right now you don't understand."

B

"No, by Zeus," said Cebes, "not by a long shot!"

"But," said he, "all I mean is this — nothing new but the very thing I've never stopped talking about at other times and in the account that's just occurred as well. For I'm going to try to show you the form of the cause with which I've busied myself. And I'll go back to those much-babbled-about things and take my beginning from them, putting down as hypothesis that there's some Beautiful Itself by Itself and a Good and a Big and all the others. If you give me those and grant that they *are*, I hope, from them, to

C

show you the cause and to discover how soul is something deathless."

"By all means, take it as given," said Cebes, "don't let that stop you from finishing the account!"

"Consider then," he said, "whether you're of my opinion about what comes next after this. For it appears to me that if anything else is beautiful besides the Beautiful Itself, it's not beautiful because of any other single thing but this: because it participates in that Beautiful. And I speak of all things in this way. Do you grant such a cause?"

"I grant it," he said.

D

"Therefore I no longer understand," said he, "nor am I able to recognize the other causes — those wise ones. But if somebody should tell me why anything is beautiful by saying it has a blossoming color or shape or anything else of that sort, I bid farewell to all that, since I'm discombobulated by all these other things; and simply and artlessly and perhaps naively, I hold this close to myself: that nothing makes a thing beautiful but the presence of or communion with that Beautiful — or however and in whatever way you say it happens. As for that, I don't yet make any

E

definite assertion, but I do assert that it's by the Beautiful that all beautiful things are beautiful. For that seems to me to be the safest way to answer for both myself and another. And by holding tight to this, I think I won't ever fall down, but it'll prove safe for myself and for anyone else to answer that beautiful things are beautiful by the Beautiful. Or doesn't that seem so to you?"

"It does seem so."

"And big things are big — and bigger things, bigger — by Bigness, and littler things are littler by Smallness?"

"Yes."

101A

"And therefore you wouldn't allow it if somebody should claim that one man's bigger than another by a head and that the littler man's littler by this very same thing. Instead, you'd protest that you're not going to say anything else than this: Every bigger thing's bigger than another by nothing but Bigness, and it's bigger because of this, because of Bigness, while the littler is littler by nothing but Smallness and is littler because of this, because of Smallness. I suppose you'd be terrified that some contrary argument would come at you, if you claimed somebody's bigger or littler by a head — that, first of all, the bigger's bigger and the littler's littler by the same thing, and next, that the bigger's bigger by the head, which is small, and it's surely a monstrosity that

B

somebody be big by something small. Or wouldn't you be terrified of these things?"

And Cebes, with a laugh, said, "I sure would!"

"Then wouldn't you be terrified," said he, "to assert that ten things are more than eight by two and exceed them because of this cause but not by Multitude and because of Multitude? And that the double foot's bigger than the single one by half but not by Bigness? For I suppose there's the same terror."

"Of course," he said.

"And what about this: When a one has been added to a one or has been divided up, wouldn't you beware of asserting that the addition or division is the cause of its becoming two? And you'd shout bigtime that you don't know any other way each thing comes into being except by participating in the particular Being of each form in which it participates; and that in these cases you don't have any other cause of its becoming two than its participation in the two; and that whatever's going to be two must participate in this, and whatever's going to be one, in the unit — but to these dividings and addings and other such fancy stuff you'd bid farewell, leaving them to others wiser than you to answer for.[23] But you, in fright (as the saying goes) at your own

---

[23] Here and in the argument that follows, "the unit," "the two," "the three" and so on translate the Greek number words that may be transliterated as "monad," "dyad," "triad," etc. These numbers are on a somewhat higher level than the numbers by which things are counted.

D shadow and inexperience, holding tightly to that safe hypothesis, would, I take it, answer as we did. But if, on the other hand, somebody should hold tightly to the hypothesis taken all by itself, you'd bid him farewell and wouldn't answer until you'd considered the things that spring forth from that hypothesis — that is, whether in your view those things are consonant or dissonant with one another. And should you have to give an account of that hypothesis itself, you'd give it in just the same way, by hypothesizing in turn another hypothesis, whichever of the higher

E ones appeared best, until you came to something sufficient. And at the same time, you wouldn't smush things together, the way the debaters do, by conversing both about the beginning and what emerges out of it — if, that is, you wanted to discover something about the things that *are*. There's probably not even one argument or careful thought those people have about this matter; for they're so self-sufficient because of their wisdom that even though they confound all things together, they themselves are quite capable of being satisfied with themselves. But you — if in fact

102A you're one of the lovers of wisdom — would, I suppose, do as I say."

"What you say is very true," said Simmias and Cebes together.

Echecrates: By Zeus, Phaedo, a reasonable reply! For it seems wonderful to me how lucid that man made all this — lucid even to somebody who didn't have much of a mind!

Phaedo: Of course, Echecrates, and so it seemed to all who were present.

Echecrates: And to us too who were absent but are listening right now! But now what was said after that?

Phaedo: This, I think. Once all this had been granted him, and it

B was agreed that each of the forms *was* something and that everything else that has a share in them gets its name from these very things, here's what he asked next: "Now if you say 'yes' to all this," said he, "then whenever you claim that Simmias is bigger than Socrates but littler than Phaedo, aren't you on those occasions asserting that both these things, Bigness and Smallness, are in Simmias?"

"I am."

"In any case," said he, "you do agree, don't you, that the statement 'Simmias exceeds Socrates' doesn't — when it's put in those

C terms — get at the truth of the matter? For I suppose Simmias doesn't by nature do any exceeding by this — by being Simmias

— but rather by the Bigness he happens to have; nor again does he exceed Socrates because Socrates is Socrates, but because Socrates has Smallness in relation to the other's Bigness?"

"True."

"Nor again is he exceeded by Phaedo in this — that Phaedo is Phaedo — but because Phaedo has Bigness in relation to Simmias' Smallness?"

"That's so."

D "So this is how Simmias, who's in the middle between both, gets the name for being small and for being big — by submitting his Smallness to the Bigness of the one for that one to exceed it, while supplying his Bigness for the other's Smallness to be exceeded by it.[24] And at that point he said with a smile, "I seem to be even on the verge of book-speak![25] But it really is pretty much the way I'm describing it." He gave his assent.

"I'm saying all this for the sake of the following: I want the very thing that seems to me to be the case to seem so to you too. For it appears to me not only that Bigness itself is never willing to be big and small at the same time, but also that the Bigness in us never abides the Small, nor is it willing to be exceeded. Instead,

E one of two things must happen: Either Bigness must flee and get out of the way when its contrary, the Small, advances towards it, or else it must already have perished by the time that Smallness came near it. But what it's *not* willing to be is, by enduring and receiving Smallness, other than what it was. So I, having received and endured Smallness while still being just who I am, am this same small man; but that Bigness, since it's big, hasn't dared to be small. And in the same way, the Small that's in us isn't ever willing to become or be big, nor is any one among the contraries willing — since it's still the very thing it was — ever at the same

103A time both to become and be its own contrary; instead, it either takes off or else perishes in this experience."

"Altogether so," said Cebes, "as it appears to me."

And then one of those present — I don't remember for sure who it was —when he listened to this, said: "By the gods, wasn't what we agreed to in the previous arguments the very contrary

---

[24] The word we have translated as "name" (*eponymia*) in this passage really means something more like a label or moniker.

[25] The precise meaning of the adverb *syngraphikos* is unclear. It can mean "like a book" or "with a prose style" or even "like a (legal) writ." In any event, it refers to something formal that is written down and artfully composed.

of what's now being said? Wasn't it that the bigger comes to be out of the littler and the littler out of the bigger and, simply, that this is the coming-to-be for contraries — out of contraries? But now it seems to me it's being said that this could never come to be."

B And Socrates had turned his head toward him and listened and now said: "You've done a manly job of recalling that; however, you're not noticing the difference between what's being said now and what was said then. Then it was said that a *contrary thing* comes to be out of a contrary thing, but now it's being said that the contrary itself would never become contrary to itself — neither the one in us nor the one in nature. For then, my friend, we were speaking of things that *have* the contraries, and we named these things with the names of those contraries; but now we're speaking about those contraries themselves, which, being *in* the

C things named, give them their names. And we claim that those very contraries would never be willing to receive a coming-to-be from one another." And with that he glanced at Cebes and spoke: "But you, Cebes," he said, "I suppose none of what this man said shook you up … did it?"

"That's not my condition this time," said Cebes, "although I don't say that many matters don't shake me up."

"Then we're agreed that this is simply the case," said he, "that the contrary will never be contrary to itself."

"Altogether so," he said.

"Now consider," he said, "whether you'll agree with me about this further thing too: Do you call something 'hot,' and something 'cold?'"

"I do."

"But do you call those very things 'snow' and 'fire?'"

D "No, I don't, by Zeus!"

"But the Hot is something other than fire, and the Cold is something other than snow?"

"Yes."

"But this, I imagine, is what seems to you to be the case: Never will snow, while being snow, admit the Hot, just as we said in the previous arguments, and any longer be the very thing it was, snow, *and* hot; but when the Hot advances towards it, it will either give way to it or perish."

"Of course."

"And again, fire, when the Cold advances towards it, will either get out from under or perish but will not ever dare to admit Coldness and still be the very thing it was, fire, *and* cold."

E   "What you say is true," he said.

"So it's the case," said he, "about some things of this sort, that the Form Itself isn't the only thing worthy of the form's name for all time; there's also something else, something that is not that form but, whenever it *is*, always has the shape of that form. But perhaps what I mean will be still plainer in this example: I suppose the Odd must always happen on this very name which we are now uttering — or not?"

"Of course."

"Is this the only one of the things that *are* with this name —
104A   for that's what I'm asking — or is there something else, which is not the very thing the Odd is, but which we must still, along with its own name, always call odd because its nature is such as never to abandon the Odd? I mean how the three, for example, is affected, and many other things as well. Take a look at the three. Doesn't it seem to you that it must always be addressed both by its own name and by that of the Odd, although the Odd is not the very thing that the three is? It's not the very thing, but still the three is of this nature, and so is the five and, in all, half of num-
B   ber: Although not the very thing the Odd is, each of them is always odd. And again, take two things, and four, and the whole other row of number: Although not the very thing the Even is, still each of them is always even. Do you grant this or not?"

"Why, of course," he said.

"Well then," he said, "Observe what I want to make clear. It's this: It's apparent those contraries aren't the only thing not to admit one another — there are also all those things which, not being contrary to one another, always contain contraries. Nor are these like things that admit whatever look is contrary to the look in them; instead, whenever that look comes at them, they perish
C   or give way. Or won't we claim that three things will sooner perish and suffer anything else, before they'll endure becoming even, while still being three?"

"Certainly," said Cebes.

"And yet," said he, "the two is surely not a contrary to the three."

"Of course not."

"Therefore it's not only contrary forms that don't endure coming at one another; but also certain other things don't endure contraries coming at them."

"What you say is very true," he said.

"Then do you want us to mark off," said he, "the sort of things these are, if we can?"

"Of course."

D   "Then Cebes," he said, "wouldn't they be those things, each of which compels whatever it occupies to contain not only its own look but also and always the look of some contrary?"

"How do you mean?"

"In exactly the way we were speaking about it just now. For surely you know that it's necessary for whatever the look of the three occupies to be not only three things but also odd."

"Of course."

"And so, we assert, the look that's contrary to whatever shape works this effect would never approach such a thing."

"No, it wouldn't."

"And the 'Odd' shape worked this effect?"

"Yes."

"And the shape contrary to this is that of the Even?"

"Yes."

E   "Therefore the look of the Even will never reach three things."

"Certainly not."

"So three things have no part in the Even."

"No part."

"Therefore the three is uneven."

"Yes."

"Well now, here's what I've been saying I'd mark off: the sort of thing which, though not contrary to something, still does not admit it, that is, does not admit the contrary — for example, the three just now, though not contrary to the Even, does not for all that admit it, for the three always brings the contrary to bear against it, as does the two against the Odd and fire against the Cold, and as do a great many other things. Now see if this is how you'd mark it off: The contrary isn't alone in not admitting its contrary; there's also what brings some contrary to bear on that thing that comes at it; in other words, there's the thing itself that brings some contrary to bear, which thing never admits the contrariety of the thing it brings its contrary to bear on. Go back and recollect — it does no harm to hear it often. Five things won't admit the idea of the Even, nor will ten (five doubled) admit the idea of the Odd. Now ten isn't itself contrary to anything, but nevertheless it won't admit the idea of the Odd; nor will one-and-a-half and other improper fractions, and again one-half, one-third and all such simple fractions, admit the idea of the Whole — if you follow me and it seems this way to you too."

B

"It seems very much that way to me too," he said, " and I do follow you."

"Then go back," he said, "and speak to me from the beginning. And don't answer me with the term I use to pose the question but by imitating me as follows. I now give an answer beyond the first one I spoke of — that safe one — since I see another safety coming out of what we're saying right now. If you should ask me what comes to be in the body by which that body will be hot, I won't give that safe and unlearned answer and say that it's Hotness; instead I'll give the fancier one coming out of what we were discussing just now and say that it's fire. Nor when you ask what comes to be in a body by which that body will be sick, will I say that it's Sickness but rather that it's fever. Nor when you ask what comes to be in a number by which that number will be odd, will I say that it's Oddness but rather that it's the unit, and so on for other things. But see if you now know sufficiently what I want to say."

C

"Entirely sufficiently," he said.

"Then answer," said he. "What comes to be in a body by which that body will be living?"

"It's soul," he said.

D

"And isn't this always the case?"

"Why, of course," said he.

"Then does soul always come on the scene bringing Life to bear on whatever she herself occupies?"

"Of course that's how she comes on the scene," he said.

"Is there some contrary to Life — or isn't there one?"

"There is," he said.

"What?"

"Death."

"Now soul, as we've agreed from the previous arguments, won't ever at all admit the contrary of what she herself always brings to bear on something?"

"That's surely the case," said Cebes.

"Well, that which doesn't admit the idea of the Even — what were we just now naming it?"

"Uneven," he said.

"And what doesn't admit the Just, and whatever doesn't admit the Musical?"

E   "Unmusical," he said, "and what's unjust."

"Alright," he said, "so what do we call whatever doesn't admit Death?"

"Un-dying," he said.[26]

"And soul doesn't admit Death?"

"No."

"Therefore soul is something un-dying."

"Something un-dying."

"Alright," he said, "shall we claim that this has been demonstrated? Or how does it seem to you?"

"Very sufficiently demonstrated indeed, Socrates."

"Then what about this, Cebes?" said he. "If it were necessary
106A   for the un-even to be imperishable, would three things be anything but imperishable?"

"Why, of course not."

"Then if it were necessary that the un-hot be imperishable as well, whenever somebody brought Hot upon snow, wouldn't snow slip away safe and unmelted? For surely it wouldn't have perished, nor again would it have endured and admitted Hotness."

"What you say is true," he said.

"And in the same way, I imagine, if the un-cold were imperishable as well, whenever anything cold came at fire, it would never be extinguished or perish, but would take off and go, safe and sound."

"That's a necessity," he said.

B   "Isn't it a necessity then," he said, "to talk that way about the

---

[26] From here to 107A we translate *athanatos* as "un-dying" rather than "deathless" to bring out the pairing of positive and negative contraries.

un-dying too? If the un-dying is also imperishable, it's impossible for soul to perish when Death comes at her. For, from what has been said before, she won't admit Death, nor will she have died, just as three things will not, as we said, be even — nor again will the Odd — nor will fire or the Hotness in the fire be cold. 'But,' somebody might say, 'what prevents the Odd, not from becoming even when the Even comes at it — we agreed this couldn't happen — but rather from itself perishing when Even has come into being in its place?' We wouldn't be in a position to contend with somebody who made this point by saying that the Odd doesn't perish, for the un-even isn't imperishable. If we had agreed on that, we could easily have contended that when the Even came at them, the Odd and three things take off and go away. And we could have made this contention about fire and Hot and the rest, couldn't we?"

C

"Certainly."

"So too now concerning the un-dying: If we agree that the un-dying is also imperishable, then soul, in addition to being un-dying, would be imperishable too. But if not, we'd need another argument."

D

"But we don't need it," he said, "as far as that goes. For hardly anything else could fail to admit destruction if the un-dying, which is everlasting, will admit destruction."

"And the god, I think," said Socrates, "and the form itself of Life — and anything else, if it's un-dying — would be agreed by all never to perish."

"By all men of course — by Zeus," he said, "but even more, as I think, by gods!"

E

"Now since the un-dying is also indestructible, what else could hold but that soul, if she turns out to be un-dying, would be imperishable as well?"

"It's a great necessity."

"Therefore when Death comes at a human being, his deathbound part, as is likely, dies, but his un-dying part takes off and goes away safe and undestroyed, having gotten out of Death's way."

"Apparently."

107A

"Therefore more than anything else, Cebes," he said, "it's the case that soul is an un-dying and imperishable thing and that our souls really will be in Hades."

"I, at any rate, Socrates," he said, "don't have anything else to say against these claims, nor do I in any way distrust our arguments. But if Simmias here or anybody else has something to say, he'd do well not to remain silent — I don't know to what better occasion somebody could put off the discussion than the one before us right now, if he wanted to say or hear something about such matters."

"To be sure," said he, Simmias, "I'm certainly not in a position to be at all distrustful any longer, given what's being argued.

B   And yet I'm compelled — both by the bigness of what our arguments are about, and because I hold our human weakness in dishonor — to have some lingering distrust within myself concerning what's been said."

"Not only that, Simmias," said Socrates. "What you say is good, but also our very first hypotheses — even if to all of you they're trustworthy — must nevertheless be looked into for greater surety. And if you sort them out sufficiently, you will, as I think, be following up the argument as much as it's possible for a human being to follow it. And should this very thing become sure, you'll search no further."

"What you say is true," he said.

C   "And yet, gentlemen," he said, "it is just to keep this in mind: If the soul is indeed deathless, she's in need of care, not only for this time in which what we call 'being alive' goes on, but for time as a whole; and the risk now would seem to be dreadful, if somebody is careless of his soul. For if death were freedom from time as a whole, it would be a godsend for bad men, who in death would be at once set free — along with the soul — from their body and their own vice. But now, since it's apparent that she's

D   deathless, there'd be no other refuge for her from bad things nor any safety except for her to become as good and as thoughtful as possible. For the soul goes into Hades with nothing else except her education and nurture, which things are said to be of the greatest benefit or harm to the man who's met his end — right from the beginning of his journey There. Here's how it's told: After each man has met his end, the spirit of each — the very spirit assigned to him while alive — attempts to lead him into a certain region, a region where the dead, who've been collected together and who've submitted themselves to justice, must begin their jour-

E   ney to Hades, in the company of that guide who's been appointed to transport the people from here to There. And once they've encountered There what they must encounter, and have stayed for

108A the needed time, another guide conveys them back here again over the course of many — and long — circuits of time. And consequently the journey is not as Aeschylus' Telephus says it is. *He* claims that a simple path takes you to Hades; but to me it appears to be neither simple nor one — for there'd be no need of guides, since no one, I suppose, would stray anywhere if there were only one way. But as it stands, the way seems to have many branchings into two and also three ways. I say this taking my proof from the rites and lawful ceremonies practised here. Now the soul that's both orderly and thoughtful follows along and isn't ignorant of her circumstances; but, just as I was saying before, the soul that's in a condition of desire for the body, once she's

B fluttered around her body and the visible region for a long time, goes off with much resisting and much suffering, led away by force and with difficulty by her appointed spirit. And as for the soul that arrives where the others are, the one that's impure and has done something impure, either by perpetrating unjust manslaughters or by bringing about some other things of this sort that happen to be akin to these and are deeds of kindred souls — every other soul flees this one and turns away from her, and is willing to become neither fellow-journeyer nor guide. And she

C wanders around all by herself, lost in a state of total perplexity, until certain periods of times have passed, and, once they're over, she's carried under pain of necessity to the dwelling that's fitting for her. But the soul that's gone through life pure and sensible meets up with gods for fellow-journeyers and guides; and each dwells in the region that befits her. And many and wondrous are the Earth's regions, and Earth Itself is neither of the sort nor of the size it's held to be in the opinion of those who usually speak about Earth, as I've been persuaded by somebody."

D   And Simmias said, "What are you saying, Socrates? Of course, I've heard many things about Earth myself, but not those things that persuade you; so it'd be a pleasure for me to hear."

"Well, Simmias, it doesn't seem I'll need the art of Glaucus to recount what they are. But to show that they're true — that does appear to me too difficult for Glaucus' art.[27] And perhaps I wouldn't be up to it, and along with that, even if I had the knowledge, it seems to me that my life, Simmias, isn't long enough for the argument! Nevertheless, as for what I've been persuaded the

---

[27] The "art of Glaucus" is a proverbial phrase for expertise. It may refer to Glaucus of Samos, who was said to be the inventor of welding.

E   look of the Earth is like, as well as its regions, nothing prevents me from telling."

"But," said Simmias, "even that's enough."

"Well then, I for my part," said he, "have been first of all persuaded of this: If it's round and in the middle of the Heaven, it doesn't need either the air or any other such compulsion in order 109A not to fall. But the self-similarity of the Heaven Itself in every direction and the equilibrium of the Earth Itself are sufficient to hold it. For a thing that's in equilibrium and placed in the middle of something self-similar will be in no condition to incline more or less to either side, and being in a self-similar condition will stay put, uninclined. This, then," said he, "is the first thing of which I've been persuaded."

"And rightly, too," said Simmias.

"And furthermore," he said, "I'm persuaded that it's someB   thing very, very big and that we who dwell in the parts from River Phasis to the Pillars of Hercules dwell in some small part of it around the sea, just as ants and frogs dwell around a swamp, and many others dwell elsewhere in many other regions of this sort.[28] For everywhere, all over the Earth, there are many hollows with all manner of looks and sizes, into which the water and the mist and the air have flowed together. But the Earth Itself is pure and situated in the pure Heaven — the very Heaven in which are C   the stars — that many of those who usually talk about such things name 'ether.' The water, mist and air are the sediment of the ether and are forever flowing together into the hollows of the Earth. Now we are unaware that we dwell in its hollows, and we think we dwell up top on the Earth. It's just as if somebody who dwells in the midst of the bottom of the deep should think he dwells on top of the sea, and, because he sees the sun and the other stars through the water, should consider the sea to be the heaven, and D   since he'd never yet gotten to the surface of the sea because of his slowness and weakness, should neither have seen by emerging and leaping up out of the sea into our region here how much purer and more beautiful it happens to be than the region where his people dwell, nor should have heard from another who has seen it. Now that's how we too have been affected. For although we dwell in some hollow of the Earth, we think we dwell up on

---

[28] The Phasis, a river in northern Asia Minor, was regarded as the eastern boundary between Europe and Asia; the Pillars of Hercules, hills guarding the modern Straits of Gibraltar, marked the western end of the Mediterranean Sea.

top of it, and we call the air 'heaven,' thinking that because the stars travel in it, it's Heaven. It's the same thing: Because of weakness and slowness we're not able to pass through to the outermost air. For if somebody should go to its surface or become winged and fly up, he'd leap up and take a look — just as fish here leap up out of the sea and see what's here, that's also how somebody might take a look at what's there. And if the nature in him were sufficient to endure seeing the sight, he'd recognize that *that* is what's truly Heaven and the true Light and what's truly Earth. For this earth and the rocks and the whole region here are damaged and corroded, just as things in the sea are by brine — and in the sea nothing worth mentioning grows, and nothing, in a word, is perfect, but there are only caverns and sand and, wherever there's earth, monstrous mud and muck, nothing in any way whatsoever worthy of being compared to the beauties around us. But those beauties up there would in their turn appear to excel far more still those around us — for if it's a beautiful thing to tell a story, then, Simmias, it's also worth hearing what those things happen to be like that are on that Earth beneath Heaven."

"But surely, Socrates," said Simmias, "it'd be a pleasure for us to hear this story."

"Well then, in the first place, my comrade," he said, "they say the Earth Itself, if one should catch sight of it from above, looks just like those twelve-piece leather balls — dappled, divided up into colors of which the colors here seem like samples that painters use. But up there the whole Earth is made of such colors, indeed of colors still more splendid and pure than the ones here. For in one part it's purple and wondrous in beauty; in another it has the look of gold, and all the part that's white is whiter than chalk or snow — and in just the same way it's composed of other colors, indeed of colors still greater in number and more beautiful than all those we've seen. For even these very hollows of the Earth, being filled with water and air, themselves provide a certain form of color as they glisten within the dappling of other colors, so that a single form of Earth, continuous and dappled, makes its appearance. In this Earth, in such Earth, the things that grow — trees and flowers and fruits too — grow in like measure. And again in the same way, the mountains and the rocks have a proportionate smoothness and transparency and colors more beautiful. Of these, the little rocks here that are precious — carnelians and jaspers and emeralds and all such things — are frag-

E ments; and up there, there's nothing at all that's not of the same sort as the gems here — and even more beautiful. The cause of this is that those rocks there are pure and not eaten away and damaged, as are the rocks here by the rot and brine, by all that flows together and produces deformities and diseases in stones and earth and also in the various animals and plants. But the Earth Itself has been adorned by all these things — and moreover by

111A gold and silver and again by other such things. For by nature they appear right out in the open, being great in multitude and big and all over the Earth, so that the Earth is quite a sight for happy sightseers. And there are many different animals upon it, and also human beings, some dwelling inland and others around the air — just as we dwell around the sea — and still others who dwell on islands around which the air flows and which are near the mainland. And, in a word, the very thing water and the sea

B are to us with respect to our needs, the air is to those up there; and what air is to us, the ether is to them. And the blending of their seasons is such that those people there are without disease and live a much greater span of time than people here; and in sight and hearing and thoughtfulness and in all such things, they stand apart from us in respect of purity by the very same interval by which air stands apart from water and ether from air. And in particular, they have both groves and temples for gods in which gods are really dwellers; and their utterances and prophecies and perceptions of the gods and all such forms of intercourse with

C gods come about for them face to face; and the sun and moon and stars are seen by them such as they really happen to be; and the rest of their happiness follows in the train of these things.

"Now such is the nature of the whole Earth and of the things surrounding the Earth. But within it, encircling the whole of it, there are many regions defined by hollows, some deeper and more spread out than the one in which we dwell, some deeper but not

D as gaping as the region near us; and then there are others that are shallower in depth than the one here and also broader. And all these regions are connected to one another underground in many directions by means of borings, some narrower and others wider; and the regions have passageways through which much water flows from the one into the others, just as into mixing bowls. And under the Earth there are monstrous amounts of ever-flowing rivers and of waters hot and cold, and lots of fire and great rivers of

E fire, and many rivers of liquid mud, both purer and muckier, just like those rivers of mud that flow ahead of the lava in Sicily and like the lava-stream itself. By them each of these regions is replenished as the circulation happens to reach each one in turn. And it moves all these things to and fro, as though there were some sort of swing present within the Earth. And this swing is there through some such nature as this: One of the gaps of the earth happens to be greatest in other respects and is also bored right through the whole Earth. It's the one of which Homer speaks when he says

112A

Very far off, where is the deepest pit beneath the ground.[29]

And elsewhere he and many others among the poets have called it Tartarus. For into this gap all the rivers flow together and flow back out of it again. And each of them becomes like whatever sort of earth it flows through. The cause of all the streams' flowing out from here and flowing into there is that this liquid has no bottom or base. So it swings and surges to and fro, and the air and breath of wind around it do the same; for they follow along with the liquid both when it rushes on to the far side of the earth and to this side. And just as when people breathe, the breath, as it flows, is always breathed out and breathed in, so also there the breath, as it swings along with the liquid, brings about certain dreadful and monstrous winds as it goes in and out. So whenever the water recedes to the region called 'below,' it flows into the beds of those streams there that flow through the earth and fills them just as irrigators do; and again, whenever the water falls off over there, while surging over here, then the streams here are filled in turn, and the filled streams flow through the channels and through the earth; and when they arrive at those regions toward which they're each making their way, they make seas and lakes and rivers and springs. And from there, as they sink again down into the earth, some going around regions wider and greater in number, others around regions fewer and narrower, they discharge back into Tartarus, some far below the point where they were irrigated and others only a little. But all flow in beneath their point of outflow. And some flow in directly opposite to where they rushed out, and some in the same part; and there are those that go around entirely in a circle, coiling themselves once or even many times around the earth just like snakes and, descending as low as possible, discharge back into Tartarus. And it's possible to drop down towards the center from either side, but not beyond. For the parts opposite are steep for both kinds of streams coming in from either side.

B

C

D

E

---

[29] *Iliad* VIII 14.

"Now there are other streams, many and great and varied. But as it happens, there are among these many streams a certain four, of which the greatest and outermost that flows in a circle is called Ocean. Directly opposite from it and flowing in the contrary direction is Acheron, which flows through various desert regions and, as it flows underground, in fact arrives at the Acherousian Lake. Here the souls of many who've met their end keep arriving, and after staying for certain allotted times — some longer, some shorter — are sent out again into the generations of the living. A third river discharges between these two; and near the discharge-point it rushes out into a large region that burns with a great fire and so makes a lake, seething with water and mud, and bigger than our sea. From here, turbid and muddy, the river makes its way in a circle, and as it coils around the Earth, it arrives, among other places, at the edge of the Acherousian Lake, though it doesn't mix with its waters. And after coiling around many times underground, it discharges further down in Tartarus. This is the river they name Pyriphlegethon, whose torrents of lava in fact vent themselves in volcanic eruptions whenever it happens to reach the earth's surface. And again, directly opposite from this river, the fourth river is said to rush out first into a region dreadful and wild, and on the whole having a dark blue color, which region they name Stygian, and the lake that the river makes when it discharges, the Styx. And after it has rushed in here and taken on dreadful powers within its waters, it sinks beneath the earth and, as it coils around, makes its way in the direction contrary to the Pyriphlegethon and comes level with it on the other side of the Acherousian Lake; and the waters of this river too mix with no others; instead this one as well, after going around in a circle, discharges into Tartarus opposite the Pyriphlegethon; and the name of this river is, as the poets say, Cocytus.

"And since such is the nature of these things, whenever those who've met their end arrive at the region where the spirit conveys each of them, they first submit themselves to justice — both those who lived their lives nobly and piously, as well as those who didn't. And all who seem to have lived middling lives journey on foot as far as the Acheron, embark on rafts reserved for them, and on these arrive at the lake. And there they dwell and, purified by paying the penalty for their unjust deeds (if one of them's done something unjust), are released, and they carry off honors for their good deeds, each man according to his worth. But all who seem to be in an incurable condition because of the magnitude of their misdeeds — people who perpetrated many

113A

B

C

D

E

and great sacrileges or unjust manslaughters and many crimes, or whatever else happens to be of that sort — these a fitting Destiny casts into Tartarus, from which there is no exit. And all who seem to have done misdeeds curable although great — for example, those who've practised some violence against father or mother under the influence of anger and live out the rest of their lives in repentance, or those who became homicides in some other such way — these of necessity rush into Tartarus. And after they've rushed in and have been there for one year, the surge discharges them — the homicides down along Cocytus and the parricides and matricides down along Pyriphlegethon. And whenever, as they're swept along, they draw level with the Acherousian lake, at that point they raise a cry and call out — some to those they've slain, others to those against whom they've committed outrages; and once they've called out, they supplicate and entreat these people to let them go forth into the lake and to receive them. And whenever they do persuade them, they go forth and cease from their evils; but if they don't, they're swept once more into Tartarus and from there again into the rivers, and they don't stop suffering all this until they persuade those to whom they did injustice; for this is the judgement imposed on them by their judges. But all who seem to have distinguished themselves in leading a holy life — it is they who are liberated and set free from these regions here within the Earth, as though from prisons, and who, arriving at their pure dwelling up top, dwell on the surface of the Earth. And of these people, the ones who've been sufficiently purified by philosophy live without bodies for all time to come; and they arrive at dwellings still more beautiful than these others, dwellings that aren't easy to reveal … nor is there sufficient time at present. But now, because of all we've described, Simmias, we should do everything so as to partake of virtue and thoughtfulness in life. For beautiful is the prize, and the hope great.

"Now to insist that all this holds in just the way I've described it, isn't fitting for a man with any mind. Nevertheless, that this or something like it is the case regarding our souls and their dwellings, since it's apparent that the soul is in fact something deathless, does seem to me both fitting to insist on and worth the risk for one who thinks it's so — for a noble risk it is! And he should sing, as it were, incantations to himself over and over again; and that's just why I've drawn out the story for so long. Yes, it's because of this that a man should be confident on behalf of his own soul — the man, that is, who in his life bade farewell to the other, body-related pleasures and ornaments as something alien to him, considering them more likely to do him harm than good, and who seriously pursued the learning-related pleasures, and who, having adorned his soul not with something alien but with the

115A   soul's own adornment — moderation and justice and courage and freedom and truth — awaits the journey to Hades like one who means to journey whenever fate should call. Now you, Simmias and Cebes and you others," he said, "will each make the journey hereafter at a certain time. 'But me Destiny calls anon,' as a man in a tragedy might declaim, and the hour for me to turn to the bath is nearly come. For surely it seems better to drink the potion after bathing and not to give the women the trouble of bathing a corpse."

B   Now when he said that, Crito said, "Alright, Socrates, but what last instructions do you have for these others or me either about your children or about anything else? Is there anything at all we could do for you by way of a special favor?"

"Just what I'm always telling you, Crito," he said, "nothing very novel: By caring for yourselves, you'll be doing whatever you do as a favor to me and to mine and to yourselves, even if you don't agree to anything now. But if you're careless of yourselves and aren't willing to live, as it were, in the footsteps of the things said now and in the time before, no matter how many agreements you may make at present, and how emphatically, you won't

C   be doing much."

"Then we'll put our hearts into doing as you say," he said. "But in what way shall we bury you?"

"However you want to," he said, "if, that is, you catch me and I don't get away from you!" And with a serene laugh and a glance in our direction, he said: "I'm not persuading Crito, gentle-

D   men, that I am this Socrates — the one who is now conversing and marshalling each of our arguments. Instead, he thinks I'm that one he'll see a little later as a corpse and so asks how he should bury me. And as for the long argument I've been making from way back, that when I drink the potion I shall no longer remain here with you but shall be off and gone to all sorts of happiness among the blessed — to him I seem to be merely talking and telling encouraging tales at once to you and to me. So give a pledge for me before Crito," he said, "the pledge contrary to the one *he* made before the judges. For he swore that I would remain here. But as for you: Give a pledge that I shall by no means

E   remain here when I die, but shall be off and gone, so that Crito may bear it more easily and, as he sees my body being either burnt or buried, won't make a fuss over me because he thinks I'm suffering dreadfully, nor say at the funeral that he's laying out Socrates, or carrying him to his grave or burying him. For know this well, my excellent Crito," said he, "that not to speak in a fine way not only strikes a false note in itself, but also makes for something bad in our souls. Instead, you should be confident and declare that you're burying my body, and you should bury it just as seems agreeable to you and as you think is most in accordance with custom."

116A

When he had said this, he got up to go into a sort of chamber to bathe, and Crito followed him and kept telling us to wait behind. So we waited, conversing among ourselves and examining closely what had been said, and then again going through our misfortune — how great it would be — since we simply believed that we'd spend the rest of our life just like orphans robbed of their father. But when he'd bathed and his children had been brought to him — two of his sons were small, and one big — and when those women who belong to his household had arrived, then once he'd conversed with them in front of Crito and had given the instructions he wished to, he told the women and children to go away, and he himself came to us. And it was already close to the setting of the sun (he'd spent much time within). Once he had come, he sat down, freshly bathed, and after this not many things were discussed. And the servant of the Eleven came and stood by him and said, "Socrates, I certainly won't pass the same judgment on you that I pass on others: They get angry with me and curse me when I order them to drink the potion under the compulsion of the officials. But as for you, during this time I've come to recognize you as the noblest and gentlest and best man among those who've ever arrived here; what's more, I know well that you're angry not with me but with those others — for you recognize who's responsible. So now — for you know what I came to report — farewell and try to bear these necessities as easily as possible." And bursting into tears as he turned around, he began to walk away.

B

C

D

And Socrates, as he glanced up at him, said, "Farewell to you, too, and we'll do as you say." And with that he said to us, "How civilized that human being is; indeed, throughout my whole time here he used to visit me and sometimes used to converse with me and was the choicest of men — and now see how nobly he weeps for me. But come now, Crito, let us be persuaded by him, and let somebody bring in the potion, if it's been concocted, and if it hasn't been, let the man concoct it."

E   And Crito said, "But Socrates, I think there's still sun on the mountains and it hasn't set yet. Also, I know that others drink very late, long after the order comes to them, and after they've dined and drunk very well, and even after some have had inter-course with anyone they happen to desire. So don't hurry — there's still a ways to go."

And Socrates said, "It's reasonable for those you mention, Crito, to do these things — they suppose they profit by doing them — and it's reasonable that I won't. For I don't think I'll profit at all by drinking a little later — except, of course, to make myself a laughingstock in my own eyes by clinging to life and being stingy with it when there's nothing more left. So come on," he said, "be persuaded and don't act otherwise!"

117A

And Crito, when he heard this, nodded to the boy who was standing nearby. And the boy, after he'd gone out and spent a long time away, came back bringing the one who was to give the potion, which he carried, already concocted, in a cup. When Socrates saw the man, he said, "Alright, best of men, since you're one who has knowledge of these things, what should I do?"

"Nothing," he said, "other than drink and walk around until you get heavy in the legs and then lie down; and the potion will act of itself." And with that, he extended the cup to Socrates.

B

And having taken it — and very graciously too, Echecrates — without the least tremor and without any falling off in his color or expression, but instead, looking up from under his brows at the man with that bull's look that was so usual with him, he said, "What do you say to pouring somebody a libation from this drink? Is it allowed, or not?"

"Socrates," he said, "we concoct only so much as we think is the right dose to drink."

C

"I understand," said he, "but I suppose I am allowed to, and indeed should, pray to the gods that my emigration from here to There may turn out to be a fortunate one. That's just what I'm praying for — and may it be so!" And with these words he put the cup to his lips and downed it with great readiness and relish. Now up to that point, most of us had been fairly able to keep ourselves from weeping. But when we saw that he was drinking — indeed, that he had drunk — we could do so no longer. In spite of myself, my own tears poured forth in torrents, so that I

hid my face and bewailed my loss — for it was not him I bewailed, oh no, but my own misfortune ... to be robbed of such a
man for a comrade! Crito got up and left even before I did, since
he couldn't keep back his tears. But Apollodorus, who hadn't
stopped weeping even during the whole time before, at that moment really let loose with such a storm of wailing and fussing
that there wasn't a single one of those present whom he didn't
break up — except, of course, Socrates himself.

And that man said, "What are you doing, you wonders! Surely
this wasn't the least of my reasons for sending the women away
— so they wouldn't strike such false notes! For I've heard too
that one should meet one's end in propitious silence. So be still
and control yourselves!"

And when we heard this, we grew ashamed of ourselves and
held back our weeping. He walked around, and when he said his
legs had gotten heavy, he lay down on his back — that's what the
man told him to do — and with that, the one who'd given him
the potion laid hold of him and, after letting some time elapse,
began examining his feet and legs, and then gave his foot a hard
pinch and asked him if he sensed it — he said "no" — and again,
after that, his thighs. And going upward in this way, he showed
us that he was growing cold and stiff. And he himself touched
him and said that when it came to his heart, at that point he'd be
gone.

And the parts about his lower belly had already nearly grown
cold when he uncovered himself (for he had covered himself)
and said what was to be the final thing he uttered: "Crito," he
said, "we owe a cock to Asclepius. So pay the debt and don't be
careless."

"Very well, it shall be done," said Crito, "but see if you have
anything else to say."

When he asked him this, he no longer answered. But after he
let a little time elapse, he moved, and the man uncovered him,
and he'd composed his countenance; and when Crito saw this,
he closed his mouth and his eyes.

This was the end, Echecrates, of our comrade, as it came to
pass — a man, as we may say, who was, among those of that time
we'd come up against, the best and, yes, the most thoughtful and
the most just.

GLOSSARY

The entries in this glossary are grouped not alphabetically but according to associated meanings. Our hope is that readers will use the glossary not only to find out our translation of Greek words — many of which are recognizable in transliteration — but also as an introduction to the basic vocabulary of philosophical inquiry.

The accents that appear are stress marks.

*****

speech, **account** or **argument** (*lógos*)

The Greek verb *legein* ordinarily means say or speak, but its root meaning is gather or select. (See, for instance, 59D and 107D.) Hence the noun derived from it, *logos*, means everything from sentence (the gathering together in speech of subject and predicate) to account (a discerning tallying up of pros and cons) to argument (a skilful marshalling of reasons in support of a position) to reason (in the sense of rational principle) to ratio (a determinate relation between numbers or magnitudes). We translate *logos* as "speech," "account" or "argument" and *legein* as "say," "speak," "mean" or "put" (as in "Well put!").

The verb *logizesthai* and the corresponding noun *logismos*, both derived from *logos*, tend to underscore the calculative or mathematical aspects of *logos*. We translate *logizesthai* as "reason," "calculate" or "reckon," and *logismos* as "reasoning" or "reckoning." *Dia-legesthai*, to talk things through, is "converse," "discuss" or "talk with"; *homologein*, to speak alike or say the same thing, is "agree." Finally, *apo-logeisthai* (literally, speak away) means not, as one might expect, apologize, but defend, that is, ward off in speech. We translate *apologeisthai* as "make a defense" and *apologia*, the corresponding noun, as "defense."

knowledge (*epistéme*), **know** (*eidénai*), **recognize** (*gignóskein*), **mind** (*nous*), **thought** (*diánoia*), **notion** (*énnoia*)

A wide range of terms are used in the *Phaedo* to characterize knowledge, knowing and coming to know. *Episteme* is the Greek word for knowledge in the sense of an assured, articulable understanding of a specific subject matter, for knowledge one can stand or rest on (*ep-istasthai*). We always translate *episteme* as "knowledge" and its corresponding verb, *epistasthai*, as "have knowledge." The verb *gignoskein* — related to our words "know" and "cognition" — suggests knowledge and judgement born of deep intimacy and familiarity with persons and things. "Recognize" is our translation for *gignoskein*.

The sense of touch lies at the root of yet another set of knowledge words: *lambanein*, which we translate as "catch" or "grasp" and *haptein*, which we translate in different contexts as "lay hold of," "get in touch with" and "have contact with."

But by far the greatest number of words for knowledge stem from four words for seeing. *Eidenai*, the perfective form of *horan*, see, we translate as "know" — to know is to have seen. Related to *noein*, to perceive with the eye or mind's eye, are the nouns *nous*, "mind," *dianoia*, "thought" and *ennoia*, "notion;" and the verbs *katanoein*, "detect," *dianoeisthai*, "think," "think through" or "keep in mind," and *ennoein*, "note," "take note," "notice" or "get the notion."

Skopein and *skeptesthai* — consider the English "scope" and "skeptic" — we translate as "see," "look at," "look into," "examine" or "investigate." Finally, *theasthai* and *theorein* are "behold" in the body of the dialogue and "see the sight" or "catch sight of" in the myth. The related noun, *theoria* (often rendered as contemplation in translations of Aristotle), is "embassy" — a "viewing" of divine matters — in the opening of the dialogue; *theama* and *theates* are "sight" and "sightseer" in the myth at the end.

inquiry (*historía*), **searching** (*zétesis*), **way of proceeding** (*méthodos*), **perplexity** (*aporía*)

In addition to the *skepsis* words mentioned above, three terms for inquiry turn up in the *Phaedo*. *Historia* (whence our "history") is from the same verb of sight as *eidos* and *idea*, "form" and "look" (see below). We translate it as "inquiry." *Zetein* and *zetesis* are "search" and "searching"; here the emphasis is less on careful looking than on thinking through a problem or question. *Methodos*, which we translate as "way of proceeding," is composed of two elements, "after" (*meta*) and "way" (*hodos*). A *methodos* is not a rule-governed procedure in the modern sense but simply a path one takes in pursuit of something, a way of going after it. In contrast to other inquiry words, it inevitably calls up the image of motion from place to place.

Bodily motion is also at the root of an important set of terms for stymied inquiry. *Aporia* — from *poros*, originally a way or means for passing through difficult territory — means waylessness, an utter lack of resources or, in the case of inquiry, an intellectual impasse (as when we say, "I'm getting nowhere with this question"). We translate *aporia* as "perplexity" and the corresponding verb, *aporein*, as "be perplexed"; the related verb, *poreuesthai*, and noun, *synemporos*, are "journey" and "fellow journeyer."

hypothesis (*hypóthesis*)

The origin of *hypothesis* is the verb *tithenai*, which means set, put or place. When used of speech and thought, it means put forward a claim or posit. *Hypo-tithenai* means place under or provide a foundation or support for something. When used of speech and thought, it can mean assume or suppose. A hypothesis, then, is a ground — either an underpinning or support for some set of things, or a supposition or basis for some argument or claim.

memory (*mnéme*), **recollection** (*anámnesis*), **truth** (*alétheia*)

Mneme, "memory " — related to our English "mind" and "memory" — forms the root for a whole series of words in the dialogue: *mimneskesthai*, "remember," *hypomimneskesthai*, "remind," *apomnemoneuein*, "recall," and most importantly, *anamimneskesthai*, "recollect," and *anamnesis*, "recollection." The *ana* in *anamimneskesthai* and *anamnesis* means back or again: to recollect is to remember again, to bring back to mind what has slipped away. The activity of recollecting is thus bound up with *lethe*, forgetting, that is, with *lanthanein*, "be unaware." *Lanthanein*, in turn, is possibly connected with the Greek word for truth, *aletheia*, the negation of *lethe*: The truth, in Greek, is that which is un-forgotten.

* * * * *

Being (*ousía*), **beings** or **the things that are** (*ta ónta*), **form** (*éidos*), **look** (*idéa*)

The word "Being" renders *ousia*, a noun formed from the feminine participle of the verb "to be." It is that by sharing in which, things are what they are. The nominalized neuter participle, *to on*, is translated as "a being" or "that which *is*" or "what *is*," and the plural as "beings" or "the things that *are*." These latter may be embodied things.

"Form" renders *eidos*, a word derived from a verb for seeing; it means the aspect or look things display, as well as the invisible, intelligible source that gives them their look. "Look" renders *idea*, a word similarly derived. Socrates plays on the paradoxical invisiblity of *eidos* and *idea* by making a jingle on the name of the underworld where souls are disembodied: *Haides* and *aïdes*, "Hades — the Unseen" (80D, 81C-D). *Morphe*, "shape," which in Greek often means physical shape, is in this dialogue coordinated with *idea*, "look" (104D). "Class" translates *genos*, a group of individuals having a common origin.

Socrates refers to the forms and looks of thought in a variety of slightly varying constructions. Besides the phrase "the Equal Itself" (*auto to ison*) or "the Beautiful Itself" (*auto to kalon*), he often lengthens the expression for emphasis: "the Equal Itself, the Beautiful Itself, each thing itself that *is*" (*auto to ison, auto to kalon, auto hekaston ho estin*) or just "that which *is*" (*to ho estin*). Note that our translation of these lengthened formulas differs from most in bringing out the enduring being rather than the whatness of the form.

becoming (*génesis*), come to be (*gígnesthai*)

The noun *genesis*, derived from the verb *gignesthai*, refers to process, begetting and origination. It has been translated as "becoming" and "birth." In its broadest meaning as process, *genesis* embraces both coming to be and passing away. The verb *gignesthai* has been rendered in various ways. These include "come to be," "be born," "happen," "turn out," "take place" and "come to pass." Both noun and verb are related to our English "genus," "gender" and "generate." *Paragignesthai* occurs often in the dialogue. It is simply the verb with the prefix *para*, the basic meaning of which is alongside of. Although *paragignesthai* has been rendered "be present," it also suggests being on hand for aid and support.

do or make (*poiéin*), be affected (*páschein*)

Poiein and *paschein* are correlative terms and mean, respectively, doing and being done to. *Poiein* also means make, and is the basis for the Greek words *poiesis* (poetry), *poiema* (poem) and *poietes* (poet). *Paschein*, being done to, occurs often in the dialogue and has been translated as "suffer," "be affected," "undergo" and "experience." The noun *pathos*, which derives from *paschein* and is the origin of our English "pathos," refers generally to a passive condition, affection or misfortune. It has been translated as "affection," "experience" and "condition."

cause (*aitía, áition*), responsible (*áitios*), hold responsible (*epaitiásthai*), blame (*aitiásthai*)

The nouns *aitia* and *aition* both mean not only cause but also origin, ground and occasion. In its negative sense, an *aitia* is charge, blame or accusation. *Aitia* and *aition* have been rendered "cause," but the reader must bear in mind (especially in reading about Socrates' youthful pursuit of the cause of becoming) the strong legal implications of the word. The adjectival form *aitios* has been translated "responsible," the verb *epaitiasthai* as "hold responsible," and the verb *aitiasthai* as "blame" and "put the blame on."

* * * * *

beautiful (*kalós*), **order** (*kósmos*), **order** (*kosméin*), **put in order** (*diakosméin*), **orderly** (*kósmios*)

The Greek word for beautiful, *kalos*, also means fine, appropriate and noble. It and its corresponding adverbial form have been translated in accordance with this range of meaning.

The noun *kosmos* refers to any well or beautifully ordered whole, including the world itself. Related in meaning to the adjective *kalos*, it is both ornament and decency of character and behavior. There is no good English equivalent. We have translated it "order," but the reader must remember that *kosmos* is above all an order worthy of admiration and praise. The verbs *kosmein* and *diakosmein* have been translated, respectively, as "order" and "put in order." They refer to the act by which something disorderly has been put into the condition of a *kosmos*. The adjective *kosmios* has been translated "orderly" and, like *kalos*, has the sense of appropriate and decorous.

Two words suggestive of disorder are worthy of note: *tarattein* and *phyrein*. *Tarattein* means stir up, disquiet, alarm or throw into disorder. It has been translated "shake up." *Phyrein* means both knead and mix up. Its general sense is that of mixing something wet with something dry. We have rendered this interesting word with the colloquial "smush."

music (*mousiké*), **tuning** (*harmonía*), **tune** (*harmózein*)

Mousike or "music" is any art over which the Muses preside, especially poetry that is sung. It refers, more generally, to what we would call the liberal arts. The noun *harmonia* derives from the verb *harmozein*, which has the general meaning of fit together, join and set in order or arrange. (In its reflexive form the verb can mean join to oneself or marry.) More specifically, *harmozein* refers to the act of tuning a musical instrument, and it is this meaning that proves central to the dialogue's concern for the soul. A *harmonia* is generally any means by which things are joined together, whether the planks of a ship, the stones of a building, the bones of the body or the partners of an agreement. As with *harmozein*, the dominant meaning of *harmonia* in the dialogue is musical. A *harmonia* in Greek is not harmony in the modern sense of the term: It does not refer to the theory of chords and part-singing. A *harmonia* is a tuning: both the act itself of tuning and the well-ordered result of this act, that is, a scale. It can also refer to any one of the so-called Greek modes or musical characters, which Socrates takes up in the *Republic*.

* * * * *

care (*meléte*), **care for** (*meletán*), **put one's heart into** (*prothyméisthai*), **be confident** (*tharréin*), **courage** (*andréia*), **danger** or **risk** (*kíndynos*)

There are many occurences in the *Phaedo* of words denoting the serious application of effort and bearing up amid dangers and adversity. The noun *melete* and the corresponding verb *meletan* occur regularly. *Melete* refers to care, attention, practice and exercise. It can also mean care in the sense of anxiety. We have translated it as "care" throughout (as in the provocative phrase "care of death"), and the corresponding verb as "care for." (The negative form of the verb, *amelein*, occurs once and has been rendered "not worry.")

The verb *prothymeisthai* suggests eager willingness, enthusiasm or zeal. Given its relation to the noun *thymos* (whose range of meanings includes heart, spiritedness and also anger), we have translated it as "put one's heart into" and "take heart." *Enthymeisthai*, another *thymos*-related word, also occurs in the dialogue. It means lay to heart, ponder and infer (hence the logical term "enthymeme"). It has been rendered "realize deep down." *Thymos* is also related to the Greek word for bodily desire: *epithymia*. The verb *tharrein* (related to the noun *tharsos*, boldness) has been rendered "be confident;" the noun *andreia*, literally manliness, is "courage."

The noun *kindynos* (related to the verb *kindyneuein*, run the risk) occurs at crucial points in the dialogue and has been translated as both "risk" and "danger."

philosopher or **lover of wisdom** (*philósophos*), **wisdom** (*sophía*), **thoughtfulness** (*phrónesis*), **soundmindedness** (*sophrosýne*), **safe and sound** (*sos*), **safe** (*asphalés*)

It is very important, when reading the *Phaedo*, to remember that the word *philosophos* means "lover (*philos*) of wisdom (*sophia*)." This phrase, along with the term "philosopher," is used at various points of our translation to remind the reader that the philosopher professes to be a lover rather than a possessor. It is interesting that the noun *sophia*, which we translate as "wisdom," has a pejorative meaning in its two appearances in the *Phaedo* (96A and 101E). While the adjective *sophos*, "wise," also tends to have a pejorative sense (see, for example, 100C), at one and only one point it clearly refers to something positive (63A).

By contrast, *phronesis*, the Greek noun ordinarily translated as either wisdom or prudence and derived from the noun *phren* (heart, mind, understanding, sense) is here positive in the extreme. It is the supreme virtue, without which the other virtues degenerate into base imitations. We have rendered *phronesis* as "thoughtfulness," both to distinguish it from *sophia* and to emphasize that *phronesis*, in spite of its strong connection with the heights of intellectual vision in this dialogue, refers in its most basic meaning to a thoroughly healthy state of mind — to good sense and sound judgement. To possess *phronesis*, in other words, is to be in one's right mind. The adjectives *phronimos* and *aphron* are, accordingly, translated as "thoughtful" and "thoughtless."

Sophrosyne, the Greek noun we usually translate as "moderation," is a composite of *sos* (safe and sound, in a healthy condition) and *phren*. *Sos* is related to the verb *sozein*, which means save or keep, especially *keep alive*. *Sophrosyne* is akin to *phronesis* and refers to the safe keeping and keeping alive of one's good sense. In our translation it appears not only as "moderation" but also as "soundmindedness." The adjective *sophron* appears as "moderate."

The language of safety abounds in the *Phaedo*. In addition to the adjectives *sos* (which we translate as both "safe" and "safe and sound") and *bebaios* (which we translate "stable"), there is the regularly occurring *asphales*, which means safe in the sense of firm or steadfast, not to be made to fall or not to be tripped up (as in wrestling). We have translated it throughout as "safe" and its corresponding noun *asphaleia* as "safety."

* * * * *

rule (*árchein*), **master** (*kratéin*), **release** (*lýein*), **get free from** (*apallássesthai*)

The basic terms of political life, *archein* and *archesthai*, rule and being ruled, rarely appear in the *Phaedo* (although the noun form *archontes*, "officials," as the title for the eleven men in charge of executing Socrates, does appear). What we get instead is *kratein*, "master" (always used with a hint of violence), *despozein*, "be the master" (ordinarily used of rule over household slaves) and *doulein*, "be enslaved" or "be a slave." *Hegemoneuein*, "govern," is also used occasionally; the related noun *hegemon* turns up in the myth at the end as "guide."

What holds for rule words holds for freedom words as well. The language of political freedom — *eleutheros* or "free" and *eleutheria* or "freedom" — is very rare. In place of this we have *lyein*, "release" (which always has the sense of breaking or getting loose from bonds, overcoming impediments), and *apallassesthai*, "get or set free from" (which often suggests getting rid of something disagreeable or harmful).

death (*thánatos*), **destruction** (*phthorá*), **perish** (*apóllysthai*), **meet one's end** (*teleután*)

To preserve their connection with *thanatos*, "death," we translate the adjective *thnetos* (literally, able to die) as "deathbound" and the adjective *athanatos* as "deathless" or, in one stretch of the dialogue, "undying."

Apollysthai and the related adjective *anolethros* we translate as "perish" and "imperishable." *Phthora* is "destruction," the verb *diaphtheiresthai* "be destroyed" and the related adjective *adiaphthoros* "indestructible" or "undestroyed." *Teleutan*, from *telos* (end in the sense of limit *or* completion), we translate as "meet one's end."

potion (*phármakon*)

The word *pharmakon*, related to our English "pharmacy," means both medicine and poison. We translate it as "potion" because this word covers both meanings and in addition suggests enchantment. In the dialogue *Charmides* Socrates himself tells the boy Charmides of a potion against headache but says that it requires a spoken charm for the cure to be effective. There that charm is Socrates' conversation (155E), and so it is in the *Phaedo*.

BIBLIOGRAPHY

The following texts and translations were most frequently consulted:

R. D. Archer-Hind, *The Phaedo of Plato*, (2nd ed.) London, 1894, New York: Macmillan (1973).

J. Burnet, *Plato's Phaedo*, Oxford: Oxford University Press (1911).

F. Dirlmeier, *Platon: Phaidon*, Munich: Heimeran Verlag (1949).

H. N. Fowler, *Plato: Euthyphro, Apology, Crito, Phaedo, Phaedrus*, Cambridge: Harvard University Press, Loeb Library (1914).

D. Gallop, *Plato: Phaedo*, Oxford: Oxford University Press (1975).

G. M. A. Grube, *Plato: Phaedo*, Indianapolis: Hackett Publishing Company (1977).

R. Larson, *Plato: the Symposium and the Phaedo*, Arlington Heights, IL: Harlan Davidson, Inc., Crofts Classics (1980).

F. Schleiermacher, *Platon: Phaidon, Politeia*, 1828, Germany: Rowohlt's Klassiker (1960).

The following sources were of particular use for our Introduction and Translation:

Aristotle, *Meteorologica*, 355 Bff.

H. W. Ausland, "On Reading Plato Mimetically," *American Journal of Philology*, Vol. 118, no. 3, (Fall, 1997), 371-416.

D. Bolotin, "The Life of Philosophy and the Immortality of the Soul: An Introduction to Plato's *Phaedo*," *Ancient Philosophy* 7:39-56.

R. Burger, *The Phaedo: A Platonic Labyrinth*, New Haven: Yale University Press (1984).

K. Dorter, *Phaedo: An Interpretation*, Canada: University of Toronto Press (1982).

P. Friedländer, *Plato*, Vol. I, Chapter 15, "Plato as Geographer," New York: Pantheon Books, Bollingen Series LIX (1958).

A. Hartle, *Death and the Disinterested Spectator*, Chapter I, "Penelope and the Bee," Albany: State University of New York Press (1986).

J. Klein, "Plato's *Phaedo*," *Lectures and Essays*, edited by R. Williamson and E. Zuckerman, Annapolis: St. John's Press (1985), 375-393.

J. Klein, *A Commentary on Plato's Meno*, Chapel Hill, NC: The University of North Carolina Press (1965), 125-150.

S. Rosen, *The Question of Being*, Chapter 2, "Socrates' Hypothesis," New Haven: Yale University Press (1993), 46-95.

Why does he choose the most
equal as a form for equalities
that are lesser, therefore never equal?